"Blue-Collar Gold *is a winner! It's an easy and fun read that is packed with powerful information. Mark is a stand-up leader and trailblazer in the chimney and fireplace industry. His breadth of business experience easily translates to most any industry. Our country needs more men like Mark. He's a guy who's not afraid to roll up his sleeves and do the work. But he also has the vision and business chops to create a thriving blue-collar business—one that provides a great career opportunity for many, not to mention serves the community at large. Pick up a copy and find your* Blue-Collar Gold *niche!"*

~Rob Lindemann
CEO, Lindemann Chimney Company

BLUE-COLLAR GOLD

BLUE-COLLAR GOLD

How To Build A Service
Business From The Dirt Up

MARK STONER

NEXT CENTURY
PUBLISHING

Blue-Collar Gold
How To Build A Service Business From The Dirt Up

Copyright ©2016 by Mark Stoner
All rights reserved.

Published by Next Century Publishing
Las Vegas, Nevada
www.NextCenturyPublishing.com

Publisher's Note: This is a work of fiction. Names, characters, places, and incidents are a product of the author's imagination. Locales and public names are sometimes used for atmospheric purposes. Any resemblance to actual people, living or dead, or to businesses, companies, events, institutions, or locales is completely coincidental.

ISBN: 978-1-68102-107-2
Library of Congress Control Number: 2015960487

Printed in the United States of America

DEDICATION

To my wife, Terry, who has been the rock for me while I learned the lessons of life and business.

To my son, Saxon, and my daughter, Evane, who make me feel lucky to be their dad. I'm excited to see what they will make happen in life. They are great people.

To my mom and dad, who made me feel like I had something special to share.

To my brother and the StonerSix, wow! What a force of nature! I'm very proud of you.

To my sister and her family: I love you all.

John Meredith, without you reaching out to pick me up and teaching me along the way, I couldn't have run so far so fast.

To all the employees at Ashbusters Chimney Service, who have let me learn leadership and business building on their shoulders and with their support.

And lastly, to the Chimney Sweeps out there: I love being a chimney sweep, and I know you do too. Be careful and "Sweeps Luck" to all of you!

CONTENTS

BLUE-COLLAR GOLD

INTRODUCTION

*"Contrary to popular belief, my experience has shown
me that the people who are exceptionally good in
business aren't so because of what they know but
because of their insatiable need to know more."*

—*Michael E. Gerber,* The E-Myth Revisited: Why
Most Small Businesses Don't Work and What to
Do About It

Problem: most Americans don't realize the potential goldmine in blue-collar business. By "blue-collar business" I mean a business providing a specialized service requiring a trained employee and manual labor. In my case it is chimney sweeping, but it can range from construction to gardening to plumbing and junk removal. When people hear "business," they usually think of designer suits, high-rise office buildings, and meetings upon meetings. Many people who want to start a new business probably wouldn't consider blue-collar work as an option and are missing out as a result.

The service industry is huge and untapped in many areas, but many people, including current business owners, don't know how to capitalize on it. Society, technology, and the economy may change, but people will always need someone to fix, install, or take care of something in their home that they can't do themselves. If you learn how to run this type of business correctly, you will always have a way to make money.

In this book I want to show you many of the core elements for building a successful service business while helping you avoid many of the "hard knocks" that I went through. I believe that if you apply the lessons I've laid out in each chapter, you will be able to build a successful business in a fraction of the time that it took me. Just the fact that you are reading this book puts you years ahead of me on my journey through this crazy thing called business. I now know that the sky is the limit for you if you choose to build a business, but just like most business books will tell you, there is no substitute for hard work.

My Aunt Linda is one of the hardest working people I have ever known. One time while we were discussing how different people have different work ethics she said, "Mark, there are workers and there are nots!" I know she didn't mean to say it in quite such a harsh sounding way, but it sure stuck with me and has been a guiding saying to help me quickly assess someone who is working for me.

"Is that guy or girl a worker or a not?" I love, love, love workers; they are happier people in general and you don't have to tell them to stay busy. You don't have to worry about catching them milking the clock. They are content to be left alone to do their job, so you won't have to waste time babysitting them or chasing up after them like you would with "nots." These people find meaning and purpose in their work, take pride in what they do, and will work to a much higher standard.

I'm one of those people who is naturally wired to work. I just like to be on the go, trying to create something out of nothing or pushing any limit that I may see in business. It is immensely satisfying. I love my business, and I love helping others build their own businesses. In fact, I get a huge rush out of the great stories that I hear about people making big steps, taking their future into their hands, and winning.

By reading this book you'll learn how to:

1. Think bigger—allow yourself to build the business that you've always wanted.

2. Be a leader—learn to lead people to build a large service business.

3. Get out of your own way—the majority of businesses I consult with have a leader who is stopping the flow of growth.

According to a *Forbes Magazine* article from January 2015, between 10 and 20 million Americans are out of work, yet over three million blue-collar or skilled-labor jobs went unfilled in 2013.

A business revolution is appearing in statistics, but a blue-collar business is not as sexy as starting a new technology company, video game company, or consulting service—or even as becoming a lawyer. Even in an unstable economy, there is still a social stigma against blue-collar work that turns people off. They assume that because blue-collar workers wear dirty overalls, it must not pay well.

Mike Rowe, host of the TV show *Dirty Jobs,* said, "In high schools, the vocational arts have all but vanished. We've elevated the importance of 'higher education' to such a lofty perch that all other forms of knowledge are now labeled 'alternative.' Millions of parents and kids see apprenticeships and on-the-job training opportunities as 'vocational consolation prizes,' best suited for those not cut out for a four-year degree. And still we talk about millions of shovel-ready jobs for society that doesn't encourage people to pick up a shovel."

Do you have that burn to start a business? Do you talk about it and dream about it? Do you hear about someone else in business and wish it was you or wish you had the courage to do what that person did? Are you miserable at your current job? Do you need some type of adventure in your life? There are a million reasons to start your own business. For me, it really wasn't about what type of work I was going to do as much as it was something that I saw and said, "I can do that!"

This is my story, and all of the business and leadership knowledge that I could put down that may help you with your journey. I want to make a deal with you, though: I will pour out everything I know in an effort to help you be successful. In return, you write to me and tell me when you are winning or losing. I want to hear what is working, what obstacle you overcame, and how you are feeling. Deal? Here's my email: mark@ashbusters.net.

So here goes:

No one was ever proud of me for starting a chimney sweeping company. Including me. At eighteen, my first big obstacle was my dad. After reading a magazine advertisement in 1985 that said, "Make $55 an hour sweeping chimneys," I was interested. We had a chimney fire in our house at Christmas a few years prior, so I thought that I could be doing something that would really help people. When I told my dad what I wanted to do, he said, "You don't want to do that. There's no money in it. I know a guy in town who is a chimney sweep, and he is as poor as a church mouse."

See, my dad was born just after the Great Depression and grew up very poor, so he had a different outlook on life than I did. My parents had always supported me in whatever I wanted to do, so for my dad to shoot down my first thoughts of starting my own business was a weird feeling. I understood that he didn't want to see me get hurt or waste my opportunities by sweeping chimneys, but I needed to do my own thing.

I knew that I wanted to start my own business in spite of what I was told, but I needed to borrow $2,000 to buy the equipment to do it. I bought a chimney sweeping kit containing a vacuum, brushes, rods, a toolbox, a manual and, of course, a custom-fitted top hat!

I didn't have a clue what I was doing at first; I only knew I wanted to do it. After a few days of my equipment just sitting in a room, I needed to see if there was anyone who wanted my service. I started going house to house knocking on doors and offering free chimney safety inspections to anyone who would open the door and let me look at their chimney. I remember the first time someone called me to have their chimney swept.

I thought, *This is really going to work. Somebody is actually going to pay me for this!*

The funny thing is that even after I had swept a lot of chimneys and been in business for many years, I was still kind of embarrassed to tell people, especially those that I was trying to impress, that I was a chimney sweep. I felt that my friends and everyone else who had gone through college and gotten a degree were doing better than I was.

I've now spent thirty years as a chimney sweep and business owner. Ashbusters Chimney Service is one of the premier chimney service companies in the United States. I've built it into a multimillion-dollar service company that takes care of 300 to 400 customers per week and provides a good living for those who work there. This business has taught me a lot about hard work, dealing with problems, overcoming fear, and building a service business that generates a whole lot of money doing something that most Americans don't even know or care about.

Over the past several years, I have personally consulted with hundreds of business owners and spoken to thousands of people in the process. I have learned that fear and unwillingness to work hard hold almost everyone back from building the business they really want.

One of the main questions I receive is, "How do you find people that want to do the work?" The answer is pretty simple: build a business that celebrates successes both big and small. I will cover the mindset to building the stage for your "rock stars" to play on. Successful businesses have great magnetism and good people behind them. Once you find a few good employees, develop your leadership skills, and truly start to care about the lives of your workers, they will take bullets for you and help you to build the business that you want.

I have found that most people wind up on my doorstep and come to work for me when all else has failed in their lives. We seem like we have a mix of misfits and lost people who come into the chimney world. Once we show them that it's a real business with good leadership and that we care about them, they love the work. If you build a good work environment, then often work is the best, most stable place for some people, which helps them enjoy coming to work.

This book will not be about "getting rich quick" because, frankly, I don't know anything about that. I'm going to show you how to build a real, substantial business in an area with potential growth so that almost anyone can accomplish it.

If you are considering starting a business, look into the service-related fields. There will always be a need for work that requires manual labor and personnel coming to your home or business to work. Many of these businesses have low startup costs and very little risk because you don't need to buy a building, have inventory, or a big cash outlay to begin.

When you start this type of business, always have an eye on growth and expanding, not just keeping yourself busy. Staying busy is often used as an excuse to avoid doing the real work. People feel better and more productive when they are making themselves busy, but they are just substituting doing nothing for doing something that is truly helpful. You need to keep yourself busy, but only by doing the things that actually matter and will help your business.

The key is to get started. As Larry Winget says, "Make the decision and then make the decision right!"

CHAPTER ONE

Get On Stage

"The secret of getting ahead is getting started."

—*Mark Twain*

Anyone who tells me they can't start a business in America is really just scared to start one, so they will make up any excuse not to begin. I started my chimney sweep business with little more than a brush and a vacuum, but a whole lot of will to make it happen. There are hundreds, if not thousands, of businesses that can be started with very little money, from painters to house cleaners, event planners to dog sitters. The list is expansive, but you need to know some key principles to grow any kind of service business. This book will help you do that.

Despite starting my first chimney sweep business at the age of eighteen, I didn't always see it as a long-term career, as I initially had a different dream and goal for my life. Like many youthful dreams, it didn't work out exactly the way I wanted it to. But I did learn a lot from it. The mistakes I made and the troubles I went through did eventually lead to finding my true purpose and the life I live now, so it wasn't a total waste. But there were some embarrassing failures to reach this point.

In 1990 I decided to move to Nashville, Tennessee, to pursue my dream of playing drums and becoming rich and famous (probably not the best reason for playing music). I continued my chimney sweeping business on the side, but I was focused on playing music and hitting the big time. For many years my bandmates and I would go out and play music and then, when we came off the road, we would clean and repair chimneys in our downtime. There's a joke about musicians that says, "Do you know the difference between a pizza and a musician? The pizza can feed a family of four." And boy was I finding that to be true.

Playing music as a career was also a business for me because I was a 1099 contractor for the band, yet I had always (wrongly) considered myself an owner and an equal partner in the project. As we became more and more successful, I realized that the record label was really only interested in signing the lead singer. Even so, the stage is a very addictive place.

We were opening for famous country acts up and down the East Coast. We had also entered into many large talent contests and won a lot of cash and prizes. Our biggest was the 1998 Jimmy Dean/True Value Country Music Showdown, where we competed at the local, state, regional, and finally national level. We traveled to Universal Studios, Florida, to compete in the national televised contest. Sure enough, we won the competition and received a $50,000 prize in the form of one of those large checks. We were flying high and felt that all of our hard work was paying off and our dreams were really coming true. What we didn't realize was that we had just hit our high point and it would actually be downhill from that moment on.

Our lead singer up until then was a great leader for us. After all, as an ex-Army Green Beret, he was a natural leader with plenty of charisma. He wrote good songs and had a great voice. Unfortunately, we realized that the greater our success, the bigger his ego became. People were beginning to see another side of him. It was truly one of the ugliest changes that I have ever witnessed in a person.

We had many meetings with big players in the music industry, but they all wanted us to give up something in order to sign a deal. The rest of the band and I wanted to make the compromises and sign a deal. Our lead singer felt that he had to stick to his guns and not give up his publishing rights or co-write with their songwriters. This decision proved to be our undoing, and our window of opportunity closed. I was involved in several other bands over the next few years, but it never had the same magic. I realized that I would never really have any control of my future if I stayed in music.

It felt like my future was always up to someone else—a lead singer, a promoter, a manager, a record label. I couldn't handle that lack of control over my own future.

In 2001, I finally decided to hang up the drum sticks and focus on my chimney business. It had always been there for me, but I had simply not invested the time and effort into building it. I didn't know that much about the business side at that point; I only knew the technical side of how to get the job done. When I decided to hire real employees instead of buddies for my business, I was at a loss.

I hadn't realized that building a bigger chimney company was possible until I read an article about a chimney sweep in Virginia Beach. Jim Brewer had taken his chimney sweeping operation and had created a true business, not just a job for himself like I had done. He had ten trucks and about twenty people working for him. His visions helped me realize that I was thinking too small.

Once I saw that article and decided to build, I started attending conventions and meetings about business building. It was a whole new world for me, and I realized that the chimney industry involved many smart people from whom I could learn a great deal. I remember hearing Michael Gerber (author of *The E-Myth*) speak at a convention about "Magic Moments." These magic moments are turning points of realization that have a big impact on you and your business. They are almost like epiphanies that make everything click into place and set you in the right direction. I'll be telling you about each of my magic moments throughout this book. Unfortunately for me, the first one proved to be very painful.

Magic Moment #1 happened for me in 2003. I was working by myself, except for my trusty companion Smoky the chimney dog, on an old farmhouse in the country outside of Nashville. The problem with this job was it was a two-and-a-half-story home with a metal roof that had a steep pitch to it. The homeowner was actually in the front yard talking with me as I was working and reminding me to be careful.

As I climbed to the peak of the roof, the safety device gave way, hurling me down the steep pitch and off of the roof. I was doing everything I could to stop sliding, but I was going too fast. My last ditch effort was to try to grab the gutter. Unfortunately, it had a gutter guard and I could not get my hands on it, so down I went to the ground like a giant yard dart. The homeowner tried to catch me, but, thank God, couldn't get there in time. I fell thirty feet and hit the front yard. I was hurt badly.

I went to the hospital, and they found multiple tears and sprains throughout my entire body. I had to have surgery on my ankles and have pins put in, but luckily I was still alive. When I came home from the hospital, no one except my wife was there to help me. And she was not able to carry me. I had to crawl on my knees from the car, up the steps, and onto the couch where I spent the next month recovering.

Lying on the couch gave me time to think about what I was really doing with my life. I decided that I wanted to get out of the chimney business and go in a different direction. I wanted to sell my chimney business, get a lot of money for it, and do something different. But this is where my thinking was severely flawed. I thought that since I had built a good name for myself, my business would be easy to sell. Wrong!

I called around to my competitors and others who I thought may be interested in buying my business, but nobody was. The best offer I received was about $10,000, which is about $200,000 less than I thought it was worth. Mark Twain said, "It's not what you don't know that gets you into trouble. It's what you know for sure that just ain't so." And this was one of those times.

While I was couch-ridden, I read a lot, especially one book called *The E-Myth Revisited* by Michael Gerber. It was the perfect time for me to learn a particular lesson. I soon realized that my thinking was flawed. My business was worthless because I hadn't actually created a business; I had created a job. And no one wants to buy a job. One of the things that I read was that "The difference between great people and everyone else is that great people create their lives actively, while everyone else is created by their lives, passively waiting to see where life takes them next. The difference between the two is living fully and just existing."

I knew that I had to build a business that could work without me. Then I would have the type of business that had value when I wanted to sell it and move on. In my mind I was hoping that this type of business was actually a lot more enjoyable to own, even if I stayed in it, because everything would not be dependent on me. Maybe I could take vacations and get away from the business for a while. I wanted to build the business that I had always dreamed of and not some type of prison I had to go to every day.

When I consult with business owners, it seems like many of them want to wait until the timing is perfect before they launch their business or try to expand it. I am probably guilty of just the opposite—launching into something before really thinking about all of the details.

I have found that everything changes when you start moving instead of planning. It reminds me of when I used to play music and the bands would practice in a garage or living room. We could practice for months at a time getting everything as perfect as possible. The funniest thing would happen when we finally played live, under pressure, with a different sound system, a real time schedule, no starting and stopping the song, people in the crowd, and the club owner or manager watching to determine if he was going to ask us back. It was all different, and it wasn't anything like practice. Playing live took a whole different type of practice, and different things mattered then than what we had been working on in the garage. We realized that it was about ten times more important to get stage time than it was to get everything right. We had to learn how to handle the pressure, how to be truly entertaining, how to string the songs together for the crowd, how to get used to the live sound, and so on and so on.

The main idea I want you to learn from that story is that you just need to get on stage and keep getting on stage. Practicing in your garage is fine, but what's the point if you never perform on stage? It is always scary to get up in front of people who you feel are judging you, but like most things in life, the more you do it, the better you will become.

CHAPTER TWO

Are We There Yet?

"Setting goals is the first step in turning the invisible into the visible."

—*Tony Robbins*

Goal setting is discussed in just about every business book that you will read, including this one. If you don't practice it on an ongoing basis, then you can't really understand the importance of it. You actually set small goals all of the time: what time you will go to work, what you will do for lunch, what you will do this weekend, where you will go on vacation. The small goals you set are endless. You set them because you know you can achieve them without too much effort. The bigger goals that will take real effort, real commitment, and real vision will never be set by most people even though they are probably the most important.

Setting your GPS is a simple analogy about putting a goal out there in front of you. You have an estimated time of arrival, the distance, and the actual driving toward your goal. Sometimes you may have to recalculate if you get off course, but your GPS will guide you and get you where you want to go.

My daughter, Evane, was about eight years old when she was bitten by the entrepreneur bug one hot summer day in August. She came to me that morning and said, "I want to set up a lemonade and cookie stand in our driveway."

I was not excited about this because it was the weekend, and I was looking forward to planting my butt on the couch. I said, "You don't want to do that; it's too hot outside and we live on a cul-de-sac, so there won't be any customers coming by your lemonade stand."

She started begging me and crying. Then I heard it. It was my dad telling me not to start the chimney business. I immediately got up from the couch and said, "Why not? Let's do it!" So I went to the grocery store and bought the ingredients. We started baking cookies, mixing the lemonade, getting ice together, and setting up the stand out in the driveway. She made a sign to hold up: Lemonade $.50 each and cookies $.25 each. We set everything up, including a stool for her to sit on, and she was in business for the first time in her life. I watched her sit out in the hot summer sun holding her sign high in the air and moving it side to side hoping someone on our dead-end street would see it. Her brother was riding around her on his bike and having fun while she sat there sweating on her stool.

I was watching her through the front window and, after the first hour or so, was feeling sorry for her. I went outside to check on her. Her lemonade was getting warm and she hadn't sold a single thing, though a couple cookies were missing. I became her first customer when I gave her a dollar for a lemonade and two cookies. So after a couple more hours of not selling anything, a woman came to her stand and bought her remaining six cookies and two cups of lemonade. She gave her $10.

Evane came running inside, shouting, "Dad, I need to make more cookies!"

I thought, *No you don't*. But I was committed at this point, so we baked another dozen. Almost as soon as we got the cookies out to the stand, another girl came up and bought six cookies for $5. At this point my son saw her starting to make money and felt that he should be able to sell the cookies with her. I said, "Okay, but you need to sit with her and help make the cookies." He agreed, but after twenty minutes he decided that he wanted to ride his bike again.

A few minutes after he left, the first woman came back and said, "My husband loved the cookies and would like a dozen." So we told her to come back in twenty minutes and we would have a fresh batch. Evane came in, baked the dozen, and when the lady returned for her cookies, she gave her a twenty-dollar bill! It was getting dark, so we had to stop, but my daughter was already hooked on business.

She had made $36 cash in about four hours because of an idea she'd had that summer day. It was almost a magical transformation for her. She was never afraid to start any business after that. She went on to start her own company, in fact, The Little Imaginary Girl, which makes and sells jewelry. She has placed her products in about ten stores in the middle Tennessee area and even in stores online and overseas. She also started a photography business and has photographed many weddings, bands and high school senior and family portraits. She has become fearless with starting small businesses, and I'm her biggest cheerleader and business coach.

In business, every owner must set their GPS when they start like my daughter Evane did. They see an opportunity and purchase the equipment and the things needed to start. They have a plan to get going, they are excited to begin and, most importantly, they have a dream of what their business could grow into.

Once many business owners launch and get to certain levels of success, they fail to continue to set goals. So they don't know if they're winning and on course.

Every business that I have been part of has been a lot harder than I had imagined at the beginning. There were many unseen challenges and unexpected pitfalls.

I recently started a new franchise called SirVent Chimney and Venting. One of our first projects was to create an operations manual for the new owners to be able to operate their new business. My partners and I worked for many months, going through all of our best practices, standard operating procedures, software, and everything else that we could think of. We worked for many months with multiple meetings every week to collaborate. We felt that we were really working on a worthwhile project. We were doing the best that we knew how to do and were developing a manual that would serve us and our new franchisees well.

At one point during this initial process, we realized that we were off course and didn't know enough to continue. We reached out to a company that specializes in taking businesses through the franchise process. It was expensive to engage them, but we realized that without their help, we could spend years and untold amounts of money but still never arrive at our destination of creating a franchise. This company helped us realize how far off course that we had gotten; in fact, almost all of the time we had spent making our operations manual was wasted because it was almost completely useless. It was just pointless busy work we were giving ourselves to make it seem like we were doing something. This exercise did help us understand, however, the value of paying for professional help when you are entering into something that you know nothing about—kind of like using a GPS when you are driving into unfamiliar territory.

Have you ever set your GPS in an area that you know, but it takes you on a different route than you would have taken? Did you still arrive at the right place? Did you get there a little quicker than you expected? Did you see something that you had never seen before because you were always taking the same, familiar route? There is more than one route to where you want to get to in life and in your business. The key is to find the shortest route, which may not always be the one you were expecting. Something might come up while you are on the journey that will cause you to change your route, but this doesn't always have to be a bad thing. It may lead you to the right place even quicker.

If you set a big goal for your business, look for the obstacles that you may anticipate and plan how you will deal with them if they occur. What will you do if you don't have as much business or profit as you anticipated? Or what if the opposite happens and you are overbooked? Once you have identified the potential pitfalls, set a date for the goal to be completed. If you look back over your goals and objectives constantly, you will be amazed at the results. At the time it might not seem like you are getting very far. You may feel like you are doing the same thing day after day and not growing at all. But if you look back at everything you have done over the past year, or even over the past few months, you will see how much you have done.

Setting the GPS in your vehicle also lets you focus and think about other things because it basically takes the guesswork out of your journey and gives you something less to worry about. Many business owners are working as hard as they know how to, but they are not getting any closer to where they want to be. It reminds me of the story about a ship in the harbor that has all engines going full steam ahead but no one is at the helm. It may never get out of the harbor; it will bounce around and never get a true heading or get to its destination.

Many business owners start working in the engine room and they forget to work on the bridge. When I started my business, I could only see far enough ahead to fill up my schedule. Once my schedule was full, I worked more hours in the day, plus weekends, with no vacations. Does that sound familiar with your business? As I tried to add more trucks and employees, all I seemed to do was grow more chaos, more stress, and make less money than I did when I worked by myself. It was very frustrating.

When I read the article about Jim Brewer and his ten truck company and saw the picture of his fleet lined up outside of his building, it was like my business GPS had been recalculated. From that day forward, I decided that I could build a ten-truck operation. I didn't have a clue back then about how I could do that, but I did know that I could learn.

Here is a list of questions that you need to ask yourself before setting your business GPS:

1. Are you in pain with your current business position? Pain is one of the best motivators to try something different. Constant pain with no end in sight is also a sign that you are not on the right path.

2. What obstacles can you see? Make a list: money, time, age (too old/too young), employees, spouse, etc.

3. What benefits do you want from your business? (What annual income do you want? How much more time? What would make your business deliver more satisfaction?)

4. What is your plan for getting out of your business? Will you shut the doors, give it to your children, or sell it at a certain time?

CHAPTER THREE

Falling Into Focus

"The sun's energy warms the world, but when you focus it through a magnifying glass it can start a fire. Focus is so powerful."

—*Alan Pariser*

When I first started my business, I was enrolled part time in college at Indiana University. I was also working full time in a factory building automobile lifts. In business class we were asked to research starting a small business as a class project. This was when I happened to be looking through a magazine and found the ad which said, "Make $55 an hour sweeping chimneys." That became my focus for my class project, and after researching it, I became so excited about it that I went ahead and started the business for real.

I called my first company Chimney Master and had a logo drawn that looked like a muscular version of me wearing a top hat. I had the artist draw the logo to resemble the *Masters of the Universe* characters that I was a fan of growing up.

I was very good at starting projects, but I was not good at focusing on one thing and making it gain momentum so that it could achieve true success. At that point of my life I was in school, working ten hours a day in a factory, playing drums in a country band and had just started a chimney sweep business. In other words, I really wasn't doing any one thing particularly well.

I struggled with a lack of focus for many years and, because of this, it took me a long time to become really successful. In fact, my focus seemed to deteriorate, because in my early to mid-twenties, I started three more businesses in a short period of time. One was a type of multi-level insurance sales. After that I started a pressure-washing company and a vending company. I think I just found a thrill in starting businesses and was becoming addicted to the rush. I also figured out that I wasn't very proud of being a chimney sweep and was looking to find an identity doing something else.

I believe that my fall from thirty feet into the dirt helped me really start to focus. I realized that the business I was already an expert in was my way to true success. The incident with my former lead singer made me stop playing music and stop searching for something else in my life. It made me realize that I already had the answers right under my nose.

I will never forget the movie *City Slickers* starring Billy Crystal (Mitch) and Jack Palance (Curly). In particular, the scene plays out like this:

Curly: Do you know what the secret of life is?

[holds up one finger]

Curly: This.

Mitch: Your finger?

Curly: One thing. Just one thing. You stick to that and the rest don't mean s***.

Mitch: But, what is the 'one thing?'

Curly: [smiles] That's what *you* have to find out.

That trip off the roof, into the hospital, and onto my couch helped me find my one thing. I hope that you don't need a painful injury or a life-altering event to find your one thing. The truth is that it's probably all around you and you're just not looking at it the way you need to.

A lot of books tell you that you need to follow your passion and pursue what you love to be happy with what you do for a living, but I'm not sure that's entirely right. I don't love sweeping chimneys, but I did like the challenge of building the business. I like dealing with people, I like being an expert in something, I like the thrill of the whole thing and I think that's what drives me.

One of my early mentors taught me about focus in a way that I have seen very few times in my life. He was just a regular guy who drove an older truck and always wore a work uniform, yet he was one of the richest people I knew. He had started with his family auto trim business in the small town of Salisbury, Maryland, and continued to do that long after he became a millionaire.

One day I asked him, "Why do you continue with the auto trim business?"

He told me, "Believe it or not, I just enjoy sewing."

Anything that he tried, he fixated on it. He usually became one of the best people around at anything he did. One of the first things he taught me was the importance of focus. When he was in his early 20s he was interested in competitive chess. In only a few short years he became a world-ranked chess player. In his early 30s he took up playing golf, and it wasn't long before he was winning club championships. And after only four years of playing golf, he qualified for the U.S. Open. In his 40s he entered into real estate, and in only a few years he had millions of dollars' worth of property, including commercial real estate, an airport, and a bank.

Coming into contact with high-level, successful people has helped me to understand that the power of focus is possibly the greatest gift you can have in life. I have learned that I want to be the best at anything that I am involved in. I'm not trying to beat anyone else; it's to satisfy my own desire to do the best I can do at something. I have found that I am drawn to a competitiveness to do well, not just participate, as demonstrated by the two large glass cabinets in my office full of awards and trophies, from BBQ competitions to parade floats and business awards.

This leads to another issue that a lot of people talk about called work/life balance. I have never been able to achieve this elusive balance. It seems like I can focus on work and get it to a certain point, and then I can focus on my life and get that to a certain point. But I've never been able to truly do both at the same time. Luckily, my wife understands this about me and is very patient and supportive while I am in a business focus mode.

I find I'm a lot happier when I'm focusing on completing a project instead of only getting it halfway done then trying to do something else. Admittedly there have been times in my life that I wish I hadn't been so focused on business and had paid more attention to my wife or my kids. The best thing that I can do for them is to be a happy person, be successful, and give them a good role model to follow.

When you start your business, be sure to focus on the right things. I want to list them in the order that I think will do you the most good.

1. Become an expert as fast as you can. I heard Larry Winget say that you need to read at least 100 books on a topic to become an expert. Once you've read 500 books on any topic or spent 10,000 hours on it, you could be recognized as a world-class expert in the subject.

2. Get a mentor who is ahead of you in the business world and try to spend time with them to see how they did it.

3. Join associations in your field. In my business, joining the National Chimney Sweep Guild was the key to my future growth. There is an association for almost every little thing in America.

4. Become certified or licensed in your field as soon as possible. Try to obtain any additional or advanced certifications.

5. Tell your partner and anyone close to you what your plan is. The more support you have, the better off you are. But this piece is not totally necessary to be successful.

6. Try to do it without having business partners. I heard a quote that has proven itself correct more times than not, and it goes like this: "The only ship that doesn't float is a partner-ship."

CHAPTER FOUR

Major Stoner

"Leadership and learning are indispensable to each other."

—*John F. Kennedy*

I don't feel that I am a natural leader by any means. I have always said that I would rather be your friend than your boss, because I think that's just my natural state of happiness. Throughout my life I have been asked to lead many times, and it always felt like someone else could see something in me better than I could see for myself. My biggest fault in leadership is that I want to avoid confrontation at almost any cost. A good friend of mine and fellow chimney sweep business owner tends to gravitate towards confrontation. He tells me he really likes it when he starts to feel the "tingle" when a situation is starting to heat up. That's usually the place where I want to bring water to the fire, but that's where he likes to add a little bit of gas to see what will happen.

My brother is a great example of a person who I feel has more natural leadership ability than I do. As kids, we both liked to challenge authority and see what we could get away with, but he seemed to like it much more than I did. We lived on a golf course and grew up with an upper-middle-class lifestyle, but that just opened doors for us to try and see how close to trouble we could get. One summer we found that there was a way into the golf course clubhouse, and we could break in and have our run of the place at night. They stored all of the athletic equipment like basketballs, tennis balls, and baseballs for the city sports in the bottom part of the clubhouse. It was an exhilarating time for us. We would take the basketballs out on the golf course, pour gasoline all over them, light them on fire, and pass them around in a circle with our friends. We called it fireball. We were just doing anything exciting to break the rules.

When we were in our early teens, our parents went through a nasty divorce, and the judge decided to split us up. My brother went to live with my mother in northern Indiana, while I stayed with my dad in southern Indiana. Even though my brother and I fought like all brothers do, I was still a major stabilizing factor in his life. This arrangement caused my brother to go out of control in his new environment and new school. There weren't any real authority figures in his life, so he decided to challenge everyone and everything in high school.

My mother had no control over him, so she decided to trick him into taking a ride with her in the car for a checkup with her doctor, but she took him to a psychiatric treatment facility instead. During his time there, he befriended a great doctor who helped him understand that the vast majority of the issues he was having were due to my mother and the environment she had put him in. Although this seemed like a horrible way to handle my brother, he became very well adjusted and made a lot of friends at the hospital. When he was released, he had learned many tricks to deal with the stress that my mother put him under. He then decided that he wanted to join the military to help pay for college. Once he joined the Army, they helped him focus his energy, and he eventually became a great leader.

You would not imagine anybody with a last name like Stoner to be a leader of anything serious, but both my brother and I have gotten through many challenges. My brother advanced through the ranks from Private Stoner through Major Stoner and now to Lieutenant Colonel Stoner. It's been an amazing and humorous ride for him and for me to watch him become a great leader for his family, the military, and in the private sector.

I've taken a few things from his journey as I've watched him transform throughout his life. The greatest is his continuous focus on achievement. From private to lieutenant colonel, he has always had a goal and rank in front of him. Once he achieved one goal, he reset the goal and shot for another mark. His focus has led him to become an Army Ranger and a Huey/Blackhawk helicopter pilot. During the process of reaching these goals, he learned how to become a great leader as well, and I am very proud of him for it. You can read more of his story in *Family Print* (www.familyprint.org), a book he and his wife wrote to chronicle his military deployment.

My own leadership path has been quite a bit different, but has still put me in many leadership roles throughout my life. My journey into leadership began with learning the importance of reading leadership and self-development books. At one point in my business life, I was involved in a network marketing company, and one of the main things they taught us was to read books every night to learn how to build a larger network group to work with us.

I started reading before anyone followed me as a leader. This way I was learning leadership skills so that when the time came, I was prepared. As I grew as a leader, my company grew and attracted better and better people.

In the book *Good to Great*, Jim Collins talks about a leadership scale based on the five levels of leadership. He states that on his scale, if you are a Level 3 leader, you will only be able to attract and retain people who are on that level or below you. A Level 4 or 5 leader can never stay around a Level 3 leader for very long. Since learning this principle, I have strived to become a better and better leader so that great people will want to continue to work with me. I found this principle to be extremely helpful; I now have strong leaders who work with me and for me in my business and with other volunteer organizations I am involved with.

This is just one of the leadership principles I have gained from reading. These books will also help you learn general business skills and other traits you may need such as self-confidence and positive thinking. I devoured book after book while I was laid up after my accident, and they helped me gain many of the insights I needed to become a successful business owner. To get you started, here are my top ten plus one recommended books:

How to Win Friends and Influence People - Dale Carnegie

Failing Forward - John Maxwell

The E-Myth Revisited - Michael Gerber

Secrets of the Millionaire Mind - T. Harv Eckler

The Magic of Thinking Big - Dr. David Swartz

The 21 Irrefutable Laws of Leadership - John Maxwell

Good to Great - Jim Collins

Blue Ocean Strategy - Chan Kim

The Richest Man in Babylon - George Clason

Financial Intelligence for Entrepreneurs - Bergman & Knight

Reality Based Leadership - Cy Wakeman

Any book by Larry Winget

Remember, though, that reading is only a starting point. You can't just read a book and then put it down when you've finished it, you need to make a conscious effort to implement the lessons you've learned from the book. I highlight sections of each book and also make notes in my iPad or phone of particularly great things that I need to implement or remember.

Some lessons you won't learn from reading but will pick up from your experiences as you become a great leader. As I built my business and became a leader to my employees, I discovered a few leadership truths I want to share with you here.

1. If you tell yourself that no one else cares as much as you do, if you think that no one else can do the job quite the way you can, you're telling yourself a story. If you believe that story long enough and act as if others are incompetent, you will co-create that reality in your organization.

2. If you feel you have to over-manage or micromanage, it is because you are under-leading.

3. You will have problem employees for as long as you continue to hire them and put up with them.

4. The speed of the leader determines the speed of the pack. This rule applies whether you're running a dogsled team, a business, or a family.

5. Of all the people you think will never leave you, you are the only one.

6. People prefer to follow people who help them, not those who intimidate them.

7. Want to be happier? Give up the constant need to be right.

8. Make the decision and then make the decision right.

I like the Hersey and Blanchard breakdown of leadership styles; here are its four main leadership styles:

- Telling (S1) – Leaders tell their people what to do and how to do it.

- Selling (S2) – Leaders provide information and direction, using more communication with followers than the telling leader. These leaders "sell" their message to get people on board.

- Participating (S3) – Leaders focus more on the relationship and less on direction. The leader works with the team and shares decision-making responsibilities.

- Delegating (S4) – Leaders pass most of the responsibility onto the follower or group. The leaders still monitor progress, but they're less involved in decisions.

As you can see, styles S1 and S2 are focused on getting the task done. Styles S3 and S4 are more concerned with developing team members' abilities to work independently.

According to Hersey and Blanchard, knowing when to use each style is largely dependent on the maturity of the person or group you're leading. They break maturity down into four different levels:

M1 – People at this level of maturity are at the bottom level of the scale. They lack the knowledge, skills, or confidence to work on their own, and they often need to be pushed to take the task on.

M2 – At this level, followers might be willing to work on the task, but they still don't have the skills to complete it successfully.

M3 – Here, followers are ready and willing to help with the task. They have more skills than the M2 group, but they're still not confident in their abilities.

M4 – These followers are able to work on their own. They have high confidence and strong skills, and they're committed to the task.

The Hersey-Blanchard model maps each leadership style to each maturity level, as shown below.

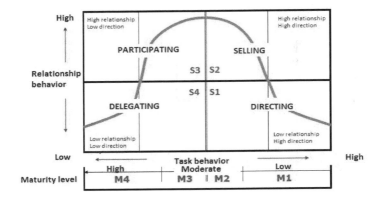

One of the key areas to focus on in leadership is being a great communicator with your group. Most leaders, including myself, under-communicate. I even do this with my wife; she will discover that I am going out of town or that I have some type of big plan, and she didn't know anything about it. Just because I thought about it, or even told some people, doesn't mean that

I told everyone who needs to know. Here are a few other ways that leaders under-communicate:

- They under-communicate because they don't realize how much detail people want.

- They under-communicate because they don't give people the context in which everyone is operating.

- They under-communicate because they are intimately familiar with the message and take it for granted that everyone else is as understanding of the situation as they are.

Leaders under-communicate because they fail to understand that people are busy, distracted, and need to be reminded. You may become frustrated when you find yourself repeating things you thought you explained two months ago.

I believe leadership is the single biggest area that you need to focus on for your blue-collar business to grow, and I believe you must do these three things to win in this category:

1. Read business and self-development books every day until you have a hundred under your belt.

2. Surround yourself with good counsel and mentors who want to see you succeed.

3. Understand your style of leadership and its strengths and weaknesses as it applies to your team.

CHAPTER FIVE

The Potential And The Pain

*"Opportunity is missed by most people because it is
dressed in overalls and looks like work."*

—*Thomas A. Edison*

There's no doubt that chimney sweeping is hard work—dangerous at times and dirty most of the time—but among most chimney sweeps, there is a true joy in the work that we do. We hear it in the song "Chim Chim Cher-ee," made famous by the movie *Mary Poppins*: "Now, as the ladder of life 'as been strung/ You might think a sweep's on the bottommost rung/Though I spends me time in the ashes and smoke/In this 'ole wide world there's no 'appier bloke."

I find these lyrics to be true for most people who do blue-collar work. They may not be singing the whole time they are working, but they really enjoy hands-on work, building or making something that they can be proud of, and serving people face-to-face. Most people aren't made to live a third of their lives sitting inside buildings under fluorescent lights in the conditioned air.

Many people simply weren't cut out to go to college or work in an office. But when we are talking to our kids or giving advice, we tend to speak to our kids in a way that portrays going into the trades or doing blue-collar work as some type of failure. Most people will say, "You should go to college and get a degree," but I don't think that's necessarily right for everyone. Some careers require a degree, and some people prefer working indoors. What works for one person won't work for everyone. With college education becoming more and more expensive, young people need to think much more carefully about whether it's the right choice for them. There's nothing worse than someone being forced to go through a long and stressful college education they don't want and aren't passionate about simply because their family or society made them think it was what they had to do. These days there are even people with multiple PhDs who can't find work, so a college diploma isn't always a magical key to success and fulfillment.

Most of our schools do not teach students about going into business either, and if they do, they don't do it particularly well. They focus only on getting good grades, following instructions, and having a good resume for when you want to get a job. This causes a problem for young entrepreneurs who want to start a business after leaving school like I did. They don't have the tools or the mindset for starting a business and essentially have to start their education from the ground up. In our economy, it is increasingly difficult for young people with no experience to find work, and yet they are being kept from a potentially lucrative employment opportunity.

The problem is that many people who are in blue-collar work don't have the training or education to lead a business, and that's what's missing in the majority of small blue-collar businesses. This is why so many blue-collar workers spend their entire lives the way I did when I was starting out. They may do their work well, have a great reputation and a fully booked work calendar, but they still won't take their lives any further. Maybe not all workers want to run a big company, and that's fine too. Yet there are many who would like to but don't think they can, or don't have access to the training to do so. These people are missing out on a lot of potential income and life satisfaction.

In the chimney industry, a recent study was done by the National Chimney Sweep Guild that found that the majority of chimney sweep business owners made approximately $60,000 per year, and the average chimney sweep made about $38,000 per year. Over 95 percent of the chimney sweep businesses had one to two employees including the owner. I then did some research to cross-reference it with HVAC companies, plumbing companies, and electricians and found that the percentages and averages were very close for all of these services. These numbers aren't great, and I'm sure when most of the people started these businesses, they thought that they would be making a lot more money. Just like I did when I saw the $55 an hour sweeping chimneys advertisement. Turns out my dad was right, in a way.

So what happened? If there is all this potential and all this work, why are the business owners not growing their businesses and not making much more money? Why are so many workers still living pay check to pay check? I believe it's because they know how to do their trade incredibly well, but they don't want to learn how to grow the business and learn the things that they don't know how to do. They work very hard every day, and when they come home, they're tired and don't want to work on the business. It's understandable; we all feel stressed after a long day at work. But this is exactly the time that they need to be reading and working on the business, and they must not stop their reading and industry education after they begin their business.

Many people have the feeling that once they leave school, their education is over, and they never have to worry about learning again. It's understandable why people feel this way, because school is hardly a great time for anyone. But this attitude keeps people from achieving so much more. We are learning and growing throughout our lives even if we don't realize it. There's no reason why we shouldn't keep on learning to fill in the gaps that school might have left.

As I wrote earlier, I ran a one-man chimney operation for approximately seventeen years, mainly because I could not see the potential to grow further and bigger than that. My biggest problem was my lack of vision for my little business. I had to learn to continuously be looking for other sources of income. What was once mainly a chimney sweeping business began to grow into a masonry repair, dryer vent cleaning, wood stove installation, pressure washing, and waterproofing business. I also expanded my territory of where I was willing to travel to take on projects which kept me away from my home and family for a lot longer. Once I saw that someone could own ten trucks, I felt that I could do it too, instead of stretching myself thin doing what I was currently doing. But I had to change my path and expand my horizons.

At the time, my new goal was to own ten trucks in seven years. I didn't have any idea of what it would take to get there, but I knew that if one guy could do it, then I could do it too.

Once I started growing, I learned a whole new reality—I didn't know what I was doing at all! I decided to put a recruitment ad in the local paper, and I was so happy when anyone would come and say they wanted to work for me. I also brought in my nephew who knew nothing about chimneys and didn't have any experience of any type of physical work. Nonetheless, I was growing and I was taking on more and more work, so I thought I was heading in the right direction.

I had a growing company, I had a few loyal employees, and I had a few bad employees too. I didn't require any drug testing, so guess what type of employees I started to hire? Oh, I asked everybody if they did drugs and, of course, they told me no, but I had a growing drug problem inside my company. I was afraid if I drug tested them, I would lose them.

After the first year, I was up to five employees, and I decided to move the business out of my home and into a small nearby office with 800 square feet of warehouse space. It was $600 a month plus utilities. I was scared to death to add the additional expense of an office and warehouse, but I knew that I could not run the business out of my home any longer.

After two years of operating in that facility, we were outgrowing it, so we found a nearby 5,000 square-foot building that had seven offices and way too much unused space. The landlord really wanted to rent it, so he made me a very attractive offer of $2,000 a month plus utilities (it had been renting for $3500 a month). Again, I was very scared to make this move, but I had ten employees, needed more space, and this was the best option available to me.

This type of growth was very dangerous because I was growing without knowing my numbers, without having any standard operating procedures, without doing background checks and drug screening, and mainly without good leadership.

My business was growing into complete chaos. It was no fun to come in to work; in fact, I would literally get sick and start to gag every morning in my shower from the stress as I was getting ready for the day.

One day, two of my employees decided that they wanted to fight each other, so my technicians went to a park to watch them fight. The most embarrassing thing was that I knew about it and did nothing to stop it. I wasn't being a leader; I still wanted to be their friend and didn't want to get in their way, even if they wanted to kill each other. Looking back, I can't believe my lack of a spine at that moment.

A funnier story that happened around that time was when my wife, my son, and I went on a canoe trip down a local Tennessee River. My wife knew about the chaos and all of the issues that were happening around my business, but she was always supportive of anything I did. On our canoe trip we came across a group of redneck guys on the river. They were drinking, yelling, and screaming as they were swinging from a rope tied to a tree and flipping into the river. As we paddled by my wife said, "Look, it's an Ashbusters job fair."

It was so funny and yet so accurate as to the type of company that I was building. I had grown to a seventeen-person and six-truck company and had surpassed the million-dollar mark for my business, but I was broke and losing more money by the day. I had grossed $1.1 million dollars but lost almost $200,000 doing it. Great job, Mark! That was Magic Moment #2.

Magic Moment #3 came when I admitted that I had built the crappiest chimney business on earth, and it was all my own fault. I had to flush the whole thing and start over, so I fired everyone and went back to doing everything myself. That summer, I pulled my 14-year-old son Saxon away from his Xbox and let him know that he needed to work with me while I rebuilt the company. He was great to work with that summer, and I will always look back on it as a great time. He learned a lot about my business and what it takes to work hard to make a living. I knew that I would still build a ten-truck company eventually, but my GPS was "re-routing" me because I hadn't been paying attention to all of the signs that I was off course. Have you heard those stories about drivers blindly following or misinterpreting their GPS and ending up driving into a ditch or onto train tracks? That was me at that moment. I was focused on the wrong thing and not paying attention to my GPS, so I drove myself into danger.

I was working over one hundred hours per week with my son right there with me for much of it. I think he learned many tremendous lessons that summer, and I'm glad we went through it all together. It was one of those times when the work/life balance thing was not going to happen. It was time to work and work and work.

There's an old biblical story about working on the Sabbath if the Ox is in the ditch (or pit). In life, emergencies arise and you have to do whatever it takes to save that Ox. If there ever was a time in my business career to put all my efforts into saving my business, this was it. I have noticed over the years that many business owners, when faced with a similar circumstance to mine, will not truly dig in and work their way out of it. Digging myself out of that hole was probably the best thing that I have ever done in business because it gave me tremendous confidence that I could handle anything in the future. It also gave me a great story to tell to other business owners who have gone through similar problems in their businesses and give us something to connect over. At the time I was very secretive about my issues, so no one on the outside had any idea of what I was really going through. It was very liberating to be able to tell my story at business conferences and be real and honest about everything. I know what it feels like to fail, and I know how to move forward from that failure. Work your ass off and don't make the same mistakes again!

If your business is failing or you are in a job that is unfulfilling, there is a way out. It's called hard work, but you have to work on the right things and in the right direction.

A few things to think about:

1. If your business is failing, are you working on the right things both day and night?

2. Could you be paying someone $10-$20 per hour to take some things off of your plate like bookkeeping or payroll tasks, answering phones, running errands, helping you with labor?

3. If you are the owner, you need to consider your time is worth a minimum of $100 an hour. If you find yourself continually doing tasks that are less value than $100 per hour, you need to get them off your task list.

4. If you are an employee, could you start a business at night or on the weekends?

5. There is never a perfect time to get started...just get started.

CHAPTER SIX

The Bigger They Are, The Harder They Hit

"Courage is being scared to death, but saddling up anyway."

—*John Wayne*

Every time my business started to grow and I knew that I had to make a big financial commitment or move to grow the business, I was scared to do it. The first time was when I knew I had to move my business out of my home and into an office with a warehouse. My office was in my bedroom, the employees had to come to my house every day, and the delivery trucks were having a hard time making deliveries. But I didn't want to spend any more money.

Once I made the decision to move the business out of my home, I never looked back. I will never try to have a business that has employees based in my home again. That move made me feel that I finally had a real business.

If you are a business owner, what are you afraid of? If you want to start a business, why haven't you done it yet? These barriers that you have are the very same ones that hundreds of thousands of current business owners have overcome to get their businesses started.

Have you ever watched the TV show *Bar Rescue*? I find it very interesting and very typical of many of the businesses I have tried to help over the years. The main problem almost always boils down to a lack of leadership from the owner. It also shows that the passion that started the business has passed or been lost, and the business is on a collision course with closing its doors.

Numerous businesses go down this road when the owner doesn't stay current and passionate about the business, or some hard life event happens and they lose their mojo. I have a lot of personal experience with this issue because my family is full of this type of thinking. My mother started an accounting firm in the '70s, and she quickly became one of the best accountants in my little hometown in Indiana. I remember her working very hard throughout tax season while she grew her business to a four-person company and moved into a nice office building. She started another phone answering service and invested in multiple real estate properties with my father. He also opened his own insurance company, and things were really moving in a great way for them. The first major setback happened when we lost our home due to a tornado in 1973.

My parents had to salvage what they could and move into a new home, but my mother never mentally moved on. She became depressed and started to take several prescription medications. It wasn't long before my parents started having marital problems. They divorced about six years later, and both lost their businesses soon after. My mother never really recovered. She fought major depression and died of lung cancer in 2005. My father never started another business but remarried and worked construction until he retired in 2006.

My sister and her husband have had a similar path for their construction company. They had built a very good reputation as a high-quality builder in our town. They worked as business partners and had created an ideal small company for many years. But as the years passed, they never really invested in their business by trying to grow and stay relevant in new building technology and techniques. Her husband would also never put the hammer down and move into the management of the company. Eventually he was injured badly on a project; his right hand was crushed between two huge pieces of concrete. Although they were devastated, I begged them to get him out of the field and to start managing the work and training his people to take the lead. Unfortunately, once he healed he went right back to swinging the hammer, and the entire business depended on him doing just that. A few years later he developed a lung infection that lead to an incurable case of vertigo that lasts to this day.

He has not been able to work in over a year, and in the years when they should be thinking about retiring, they are completely financially wrecked. I have tried to help for years, but unfortunately listening to her younger brother for business advice was not a high priority. They are great people, and I love them very much, but building a business that lasts doesn't depend on how nice you are; it matters what structure you put in place.

One of the visuals I use to underscore how vulnerable a small business can be is imagining a person on a unicycle. That was the type of business that my family had always built, and I clearly understood how dangerous those types of businesses are to operate. They are simpler to operate, cheaper to start, perhaps, with fewer moving parts, but they are so much more vulnerable when it comes to balance and breakage. As I saw the rider, or owner of the business, break down or crash, there wasn't anything left. No one wanted to buy the unicycle; no one knew how to ride it. So everyone depending on it was in financial and emotional free fall.

The next type of business is a bicycle; that, at least, has another wheel that can turn and create motion. The rider is still exposed to the elements and still has to work hard to power the bike, but it is slightly more stable.

The next visual is a car, which is becoming more like a true business. The rider is inside a protective shell, and the engine runs without the driver providing all of the power for motion. Stability has greatly increased along with comfort. If something happens to the driver, someone else can learn to drive the car. If a tire blows out, it's not nearly as much of a safety issue as it is with the unicycle or bicycle.

Finally, I move into the visual of a semi-truck. You can see a big truck that is rolling down the interstate. It has tons of power and momentum along with a high-tech communications system. Others are in charge of the routing, maintenance, loading, and unloading of the truck. It will have very comfortable conditions, and someone else can jump in and continue driving if anything happens to the driver. If a wheel blows out, the driver can keep going until finding somewhere to replace it. The semi is a great metaphor for the type of businesses I want to create. They are more valuable, they are more automated, and most of all they are more stable.

Please understand that your business will not stay the same and will not continue to do great things unless you work on and cultivate that mentality through your entire business career. You MUST stay up to date on relevant topics and the cutting-edge news of your service or trade. Read, go to conventions, network, and continue education credits in your field.

I have a hobby of competing in the Kansas City Barbecue Society (KCBS) pro BBQ competitions, and I also try to continually learn from the best in BBQ. I recently attended a BBQ school in Kentucky that was sponsored by the number-one ranked team in pro BBQ for the past two years. I love being around people who are at the top of their game no matter what they do; there's a common thread that weaves its way through people who are high performers. It usually shows in the details and in their preparation of their craft. In this class the instructor shared everything he does to win the contests—and I mean everything. He showed all of his rubs, sauces, smokers, preparation techniques, and even his temperatures and times for everything.

During the class I kept hearing others say negative things about his methods and processes. I couldn't believe it; here we were in the middle of a class with the best in the country, and these guys were not even going to try his way. They were saying, "I'm not going to cook that hot," or "I'm not going to use that type of smoker." I turned to one of the guys and asked if he had won as many grand champion awards as the instructor had or been named Team of The Year. Of course he didn't like me saying that, but then I asked, "Why are you even here if you aren't going to try everything he says and at least be coachable?" Needless to say we didn't talk much for the rest of the school.

The class reminded me of other conferences that I have attended where the speaker has had great results but someone listening shoots down their ideas. They have had nowhere near the same results but are still unwilling to be coachable. When I teach or speak to other professionals in my industry, I know that many of the subjects I talk about will be rejected as soon as I say them. This is because they are so foreign to the way listeners have thought about business. Please stay open and willing to learn and try new things when it comes to your business. The death of a business comes when you stop innovating, learning, and leading.

Here are some brief exercises that won't take you very long to complete but will help get you started with either starting your business or building it up further:

1. List what things you need to do to stay on top of your business.

2. Do you know businesses that used to be great but have lost touch?

3. Do you stay hungry and teachable?

CHAPTER SEVEN

Hey, Y'all, Watch This!

"In marketing I've seen only one strategy that can't miss—and that is to market to your best customers first, your best prospects second and the rest of the world last."

—*John Romero*

Marketing a business can be one of the most confusing and expensive endeavors a business owner can go through. Perhaps this is what puts so many people off of starting or developing a business. You can be the top of your game at whatever it is that you do, but bad marketing or not marketing enough can be the death of your business.

When I first got into business, I didn't really have any money for advertising, so I went door to door offering free safety inspections just so I could feel like I was doing something productive. I did actually get to look at several chimneys for free before finally getting paid for a sweeping. I really had no idea what I was looking at, but I needed the experience. Thank the Lord I didn't cause any fires or damage due to my lack of knowledge. I knew I had to start spending some money on marketing to make the investment pay off.

In the mid-80s, it was much simpler to make your phone ring. There was really only one main thing that you had to do—get into the Yellow Pages and decide how big of an ad you could afford. The logic behind your marketing plan was the bigger the ad, the more your phone would ring. There were always newspaper or coupon magazines, but the clear starting point was getting involved with all of the different Yellow Pages directories in your area. I remember the very first call that I received for my ad; I was so excited to feel like I was finally in business for real.

Once the internet started taking over and the Yellow Pages became less and less relevant, everything changed. And while marketing became much more complicated, it was not impossible. Yet many businesses have refused to move with the times and learn new ways to market. These businesses may keep going for a while, but they have an expiration date.

In this chapter I'm going to discuss the nine marketing methods that are working for us now. Not every single method will work for every single business, but you will need at least two or three methods to market your business, no matter what its size is. Experiment and try new things, but don't plug too much money into something that isn't going to work. Once you find which methods work best for your company, focus on them and dedicate time and budget to them every day. Your marketing methods will all work together to drum up business for your company. For instance, direct mail flyers will contain a web address, which will take people to your website, which prompts people to sign up for your newsletter. Marketing, especially online, changes all the time, but no matter what is working for your service area right now, you must always be consistent and constant.

You must market to both existing customers and to new potential customers. It is no good doing a job for a customer and expecting them to remember you. Plus, even if you are doing well, you will still need a steady stream of new customers to keep going.

All of these topics have entire books written about them. I am only attempting to show you what we do with them, how they work for us, and how they tie into our overall marketing plan.

The areas that we focus on are:

1. Direct mail

2. Email newsletters

3. Facebook

4. TV/radio

5. Networking

6. Internet

7. Print/magazines

8. Home shows

9. Fun stuff

Remember, the number one objective in business is to attract and retain customers. I once read that it costs between $6 and $10 to market to each customer during the first year, and that has proven to work well for us. It is the most important investment you will make.

Believe it or not, your customers will easily forget your business name, your personal name, your phone number, and website. It's up to you to continually reinforce your company and all of the services that you provide. Most of your customers do not know all of the things you can do for them, so you must use several methods to get your message to them.

I want to start this section with the suggestion of employing a graphic designer to develop your brand, fonts, colors, and logos. These will then be used in all of your marketing efforts, from your website to coupons to TV. In everything you do, it needs to be consistent. One of the biggest mistakes that I made with advertising was to let each advertiser I purchased from create my ad for their type of media. Don't let them do it! The problem is that everything looks a little different each time, and therefore you don't gain market penetration that you would with a more consistent message and recognizable brand.

Let's start with what we do for our existing customers.

Direct Mail: Current Customers

We contact the customer four times the first year after they use our service, using different messages on post cards. We start with a Thank You card that goes out within a few days of our visit to their home. It's a simple card that will immediately set us apart from almost every other service business that our customers have done business with. A small but effective sign of good customer service puts us in their good books.

Annual Inspection cards are recommended in the chimney industry, so we send these out during our slower times of the year. Almost all service businesses have some type of ongoing preventative maintenance schedule that their existing customers should be contacted about. These post cards should be followed up within a week or two with a phone call.

Earth Day or odd holiday cards are something that we use for our dryer vent cleaning service. We mention saving energy by doing annual maintenance on the dryer and vent. This is a great card to show another type of service that your customers may not be aware you provide.

Christmas cards, or whatever winter holiday that you celebrate, are a nice touch from businesses. Many people and businesses enjoy getting these, and it's another small notch in your belt for branding. Do not make this an offer or sale special card, and don't treat it like a card you would send to your closest friends and relatives either. Just make it a well-meaning card from your company like one you would send to an acquaintance.

We use a company called Direct Connect Solutions (directconnectsolutions.com) out of Nashville to automate the process for us and for much of our direct mail campaigns. I strongly suggest finding a similar company in your area (and it does help if they're a local company) to give your cards a professional touch. Asking a friend of a friend who did a single art class in college to save money isn't going to make your company look very good.

Email Newsletters: Current Customers

Another way we reach out to our customers is through a quarterly email newsletter. This is an opt-in method of communication through our website. We offer a $10 discount on services on our web page if the customers sign up for the newsletter before they call for service. The email newsletters are a great way to send a lot of information all at once. Many of them will end up being deleted or sent to the customer's junk folder, but we cut down on these by filling the newsletter with quality information. We will have a personal story, an informative story, and some type of discount or free gift information in the newsletter. This is probably the best way to educate your customer on all the things that you can do for them. There are many great tools to complete this task, including Constant Contact, AWeber and Mail Chimp.

If you feel your writing skills aren't good enough, you can always hire someone to write your newsletter for you, and it won't cost you too much either. But no matter what you do, always proofread your letter before you click "send." You don't want to ruin your reputation with an embarrassing spelling mistake!

Facebook: Current Customers

At the time of my writing of this book, Facebook still garners a lot of attention, and millions of eyeballs are still viewing businesses on it every day. You need to know a couple of facts about Facebook if you want to use it for your business. I don't recommend spending a lot of time or money on Facebook, but I do think that you should have a page and at least post monthly to it.

In fact, most marketing professionals would recommend posting much more frequently than that, maybe even several times per day. This may seem a little daunting, but when you think about it, it makes perfect sense. Just like with frequent television advertisements, the more often your customers hear about your company, the more likely it is that you will be the first people they think of when they need your service. Posting on social media can become addicting and time consuming, but try to find the perfect balance of how frequently you post. Just like hearing the same television commercial hundreds of times drives you insane, so will having the same person post excessively on social media (we all know at least one person who is guilty of this).

- The most common reason for a Facebook user unliking a brand: uninteresting posts (32 percent).

- Second-most common reason for a Facebook user unliking a brand: too many posts (28 percent).

So I understand that posting business facts or helpful tips is not what will make people follow your page, and if you post boring things too frequently, people will lose interest in your page. We try to sprinkle a few personal stories along with business facts, additional services, and tips onto our page. It can be one of the strongest, most inspiring types of advertising available.

My company took up a cause to raise money for a young mother of four who had end-stage kidney failure and needed a transplant soon or risked losing her life. We raised the money between our employees and visited her home to give it to her. I brought ten service trucks to her home, along with my office staff, to surprise her with the donation and to give her some "sweeps luck," as chimney sweeps are known to have good luck.

We filmed the whole event, especially when all twenty chimney sweeps gave her a good luck hug. I added some music to the video and posted it on Facebook. Within two days, about 3000 people had seen it, and she had two people volunteer to be donors! It was one of the most humbling experiences that I have ever had as a business owner, and it was all made possible through Facebook.

Social media trends change more frequently than the latest fashions, so you need to stay on top of whatever is currently popular in the online world. If it all seems too much to you, consider hiring a freelance writer or social media expert to write your posts for you. Be careful, however, of people who use words like "expert," "wizard," or "ninja" in their job title, as they are buzzwords people throw around to make it seem like they know more than they actually do.

TV and Radio: Current and New Customers

These two methods are starting to be seen as too expensive and unnecessary thanks to the rise of social media advertising. But people still watch TV and still listen to the radio, so they still get your name in front of people when they aren't expecting it, unlike Google, Angie's List, or any other type of listing service. With a listing service, someone needs to know that they need your service to even start looking for you, but with TV and radio you enter their home or car to tell them about your service or product. This type of marketing works for both new and existing customers, because the first people who will respond to you are usually people who already do business with you. Then new customers usually get the message. It will also make referral traffic grow because of all the people who get to know your name in the category.

I started experimenting with radio advertising around 2007 in Nashville. One of the biggest things I did was to advertise on the *Jerry House Show,* which was one of the most popular morning radio shows in the whole country. I signed up for the live guest spot once a week during the Friday morning commute time slot. Jerry was one of the funniest and wittiest radio personalities on radio ever, so I was always nervous to speak with him on live radio. He would never follow any script or any topics that I had suggested for the show. He would just start having fun with whatever came into his mind like my last name or my dirty job or sweeping the chimneys of country music stars. I just played along, and it became a hilarious two minute show.

The key was that it was funny and had personality, it showcased the name of my company, and the listeners could tell that I was a real, down-to-earth guy. Within six months we had become a household name in Nashville.

I had tried many different TV spots over the years and had purchased relatively inexpensive packages from TV stations. They would produce a 30-second commercial and scatter your message across many different time slots to use you as a filler for their shows. It seemed like a good deal, but it never seemed to gain any type of penetration. I finally realized a few key elements that would work for me in TV advertising.

The first was that 15-second commercials were cheaper and more effective than the 30-second ones. I would rather have two 15-second commercials than one 30-second spot.

The second key for me was to just solve one problem with each campaign. It was always tempting to try and list multiple services that we could provide in all of my advertising. Once I started using one problem/one solution per ad, we started to see a large increase in calls coming directly from TV advertising.

My first true campaign was "We Fix Leaky Chimneys." Leaky chimneys are a common problem, but people don't realize that they should call a chimney sweep to fix it. They were calling roofers and handymen to try and remedy it. I needed them to realize that we were the clear choice for chimney repair, so our commercial started with an attention-getter—a lightning flash and clap of thunder. It then zoomed down a chimney and followed the water into the house. It said, "Don't call a roofer to fix your chimney. Call the chimney experts at Ashbusters Chimney Service." We advertised on the evening news because there was always a weather story or a fire, and people really pay attention to the evening news. We placed one 15-second commercial at the beginning of a break and one that looked similar but was slightly different at the end of the same break, creating a bookend-type of look to our spot. Then, BOOM, we received lots of calls and became known by everyone, including roofers, as the company to call to fix these problems.

I have since used TV to launch or call attention to new products, and it has really been a successful method. TV or radio can really help to get the message out and make you memorable.

Networking: New Customers

New customers cost approximately five times more to attract than existing customers, so you need to make sure that the time and money you spend on gaining new customers is being used effectively.

Everyone networks to some degree or another, but what I found is that if you develop a consistent method for networking, then it can be a powerful way to build your business. Much of the networking I do is with Business Network International (BNI). It is a very organized group, and quite a bit of accountability comes with joining a group like this, so I have found it to be very beneficial. One thing to keep in mind is that not all BNI groups are the same. I recommend that you look at several in your area before deciding which one to join. Meeting regularly and having to speak once a week has really helped me with my public speaking abilities. In our meetings we must give our one-minute "elevator speech" every week. Once every six to eight weeks I must prepare a ten-minute talk for the group. I consider everyone in that room to be part of my sales force. I need to train them on all of the services I provide and what to say, so when chimney repair needs happen to come up in a conversation, group members can refer us.

Networking is a relatively inexpensive type of marketing that all sizes of companies can benefit from. It's more like farming than hunting in the sense that it can take quite a while for those seeds to grow and start producing a crop. Here are a few other networking opportunities that I try to engage in that will work for most service businesses:

- Facebook

- LinkedIn

- Lunch meetings—never eat lunch alone!

- Chambers of Commerce

- Roofers

- Builders

- Real estate agents

- Other competitors

- Local businesses that sell the products you buy for your business

Website and Search Engines: New and Existing Customers

This is a vast area, but I will show you the strategies that have proven to work best for us. First, you must have a website. It seems almost silly that I would need to mention this, but there are still a myriad of businesses that do not have one. If you don't have a website or don't plan on getting one after starting your business, do yourself a favor and stop reading this book. Please hand it to someone who is interested in staying relevant and in the game.

Your website needs to be current and active, not something that was made in 2007 and hasn't been updated since. Search engines love a website with lots of relevant content that is updated frequently. Most website platforms will allow you to add a blog to your site, which you can update frequently with industry news and stories. Again, this is something you can outsource to someone else if you can't do it yourself. Have a professional build and manage your website monthly. We use a company called Spark Marketer (sparkmarketer.com) that helps service companies all across the U.S. with their web needs. Your website needs to be easy to navigate, it must load quickly (no obnoxious Flash animations), and your phone number, email address, or whatever your primary contact method is, must be in an easy-to-find area on the first page. Most people are coming to your site to get your contact details, so your main task when building a website is to make them clear and easy to find.

The next step is to make your site appear on the first page of Google search results and other search engines. This is where your blog stuffed with industry relevant keywords will help you. You really need to concentrate on being #1, #2 or #3 in the search results for your category and in your service area. If you are not there, find help to make it to that point. If you have hired an SEO (search engine optimization) company to get you there, but you are not moving up the ranking, you may need to get a new company to help you. Google frequently changes the algorithms they use to rank websites, so the company you choose needs to stay on top of these changes so you don't have to.

This is the battlefield that you must win to have a continuous influx of new customers. Your existing customers need to see you there, too, because if they search and don't find your site, they may choose a different company simply because they don't see you. They might even think you have shut down. You most likely will never know that you lost that customer, and you will also become less and less relevant in your given field.

Another key area to focus on is to accumulate online reviews for your business. Some studies I have seen show that 92 percent of people believe an online review as much as a personal referral for a business. I have learned to trust reviews when I am making a decision about a restaurant, hotel, movie, or product that I am considering buying. With this level of trust, you must monitor your online reputation on a weekly basis. As you get reviews, good and bad, you need to respond to them so that people can see that you are active and listening to your customers. If you get a bad review, respond to it professionally as soon as possible. We have probably all heard stories of business owners who didn't respond well to negative reviews and got into virtual shouting matches with their customers. This is the best way to turn customers off of your business forever. Your response is not as much for the customer writing the review as it is for the potential customer who is reading it to see how you take care of issues.

Sometimes a negative review is correct after we screwed up. I, in turn, acknowledged their issue and publicly apologized for the incident. Most people understand that mistakes happen, even to professionals, and will appreciate your honesty and the way you react to a bad situation.

There have also been times when a customer was clearly in the wrong and I needed to state my side of the issue without getting personal in my response, even if I did secretly want to shout and scream at the customer. I do a weekly search for my category in my service area and watch what pops up. I also have a reputation-monitor service from my web company that watches across the entire internet for reviews on my business.

Internet advertising or pay-per-click campaigns are also an option while you try to get your company to rank well in the organic search or when you are launching a new product or service.

If you are using Google, their pay-per-click product is called Adwords. It appears at the top right-hand side of the search page (although Google's layout does change from time to time). Adwords works with your budget and places your message at the top of the search results page for as long as you have money in your budget. Most people have figured out that these are ads and will click in the organic sections first, but the last statistic I read said that about 15 percent of people click on the Adwords advertisements before clicking on the organic, so it may be worth your money to experiment with this method. Again, I would get an expert in this field to help you. Before I had help in this area I had wasted over $60,000 in three years on the keyword "chimney." My internet company figured out that I had wasted the money because they did analytics on the word and it showed that people were searching the word chimney, clicking on my site, and immediately clicking off of my site because they were not finding what they were looking for. It still cost me between $3 and $6 per click, but it was not driving customers to my business. The search term was too broad and needed more detail in it like "chimney cleaning Nashville" to truly get people to interact with my business.

Print Advertising: New Customers

We have found that magazines sent to middle- and upper-income households work best for us because that is our target market for chimney sweeping and repairs. The keys that I have found with this type of advertising are to be consistent and to commit to at least one year before judging if it works or not for your business. I have also found that I need to have at least a half-page ad to be seen. We make our print ads look like our commercials and website so that we have a uniform look and message. You might also want to try contributing a regular column to your local community magazine or newspaper. These get sent out to many homes and businesses, will circulate everywhere throughout your town, and are another way to build your reputation in your area.

I mentioned it earlier, but it's worth repeating: do not have each advertising agency use their own in-house designers to create your ads. Hire an outside company for your branding and have them supply the advertisers with your ads.

Home/Trade Shows/Street and County Fairs: New and Existing Customers

We set up at four to six events a year, including home decorating shows, builders shows, street fairs, insurance agents and adjusters golf tournaments. We have an attractive pop-up display that we purchased online for about $1500. This type of advertising helps to place us out and in front of a lot of people throughout the year. Another benefit is that it puts us in touch with many similar businesses that we can network with and refer business to. I have learned a few tricks to making the most out of these events that may help if you decide to use them.

1. Work the show—this means that it is just as important to go meet all of the vendors as it is to sit in your booth and wait for people to walk up to you. I have found that I actually get more work from the vendors than I do the attendees.

2. Have a traffic stopper—something that stops people at your booth is a must. I have used everything from sketch artists to golf lessons in our booth to build a crowd. It gives us a chance to talk and interact with everyone, plus it's a lot of fun.

3. Offer some type of show special or prize for people to sign up for at your booth.

Fun Stuff: New and Existing Customers

We try to do a few fun things with our advertising dollars that involve the community and our employees. One of our favorite things to do is a Christmas parade. We build an amazing float that has Mary Poppins and a bunch of chimney sweeps on top of old, smoking chimneys (with the use of fog machines) and playing "Chim Chim Cher-ee" as we roll down the parade route. Our employees and families all get involved, and the people watching love it.

Another fun thing we do is compete in professional BBQ contests as a team. Everyone in the company loves it when we practice cooking for the competitions, and many of the employees help on the team. We also invite customers and business people out and cook for them as a customer appreciation event. These are the types of things that can really set your company apart in the eyes of your customers and your employees.

The last part of this chapter will be about the budget we spend on all of these different advertising campaigns. In growth years we will spend as much as 8-9 percent of gross on advertising, but the minimum I would recommend is between 5-6 percent for a service company that wants to grow and position themselves as the premier company in their area.

I have spent a lot of time on this part of the book because I believe it is the main reason that we have been as successful as we have been. I believe that you simply must be passionate about marketing your business and tracking the results of what your money is being spent on. Marketing may not be the most exciting or glamorous part of running a business, which is why many people try to put it off or pass it over to inexperienced people. But I cannot emphasize enough how important it is. It will get easier for you over time, and you may even find that you enjoy it more than you expected.

Word of mouth is still the best referral method out there. When was the last time you tried something or used something because a friend gave it a glowing recommendation? The best way to get new customers and keep your current customers is still to do a good job, no matter what you do. But the "if you build it, they will come" philosophy doesn't work as cleanly as that, so you will always need to let your customers know that you exist and that you can provide the service they need.

CHAPTER EIGHT

Gravity Sucks

"People often say that motivation doesn't last. Well, neither does bathing—that's why we recommend it daily."

—Zig Ziglar

Have you ever gone to a convention and spent a few days listening to speakers talk about what you should do be doing, how you should think, how you can improve, and how easy it is to sell a product? Did you see how excited everyone was? Did you feel the same way? Then you leave and return home and run into the reality of actually trying to implement all of these great ideas. You have actually been visiting an alternate planet called Convention World, where everything is possible!

You don't realize it until you get back to Earth and try any of these new ideas on your business, your employees, your spouse or even yourself. On Convention World there is no gravity; you can fly around anywhere you want. But on Earth gravity is real, and everything is much harder than you realized.

Sound familiar? It happens to all of us because we can imagine it, we can dream about it, and our brains are hopeful and fully engaged. Some people decide that they would rather live on Convention World rather than Earth, so they take trips back there as often as possible to feel weightless again. They never really do the hard work under real-world pressure, so they never actually achieve the things they were told are possible on Convention World.

There are few things I enjoy more than hearing a great inspirational speaker. But I have also been disappointed to land back on Earth and try to sell what they said everyone would buy, or to try to build a team that seemed so easy for them but seems impossible for me. They also seem to have more hours in the day on Convention World than I have here on Earth. So what gives? They learned how to stay Convention-World-motivated on gravity-ridden Earth. They did all of the hard work and became strong under the pressure to a point where everything is easier. They got momentum behind them and achieved orbit but, as you know, it sure takes a lot of energy to launch anything into orbit.

Are you willing to put in that energy? You need a constant effort to get there, which starts off as a big explosion that burns and burns until you reach the desired momentum or destination.

That is what it takes to come out of conventions or any motivational situation and start succeeding. There are always a hundred things that sound great at a convention, but I'm always looking for one or two great nuggets of knowledge to start working on when I get home. The key is to start as soon as you arrive back home, or better yet, before you get home. Otherwise, the great things you heard about at the convention will be lost and forgotten and will have become a waste.

Once you hit gravity, you must brace yourself and keep moving toward your goal. Your employees will give you problems, you will have emergencies, you will face resistance from your spouse, you will have some type of financial problem, and you will be very busy and not have time for your added list of things that you need to finish. KEEP MOVING, make time, don't watch TV, sleep less, and don't stop for unnecessary activities like volunteering or anything that is sucking up your time. It is not always easy or pleasant to make these sacrifices, but this is your career you are working on, not a casual hobby. If your goal is truly important and will help you lead the life you want, put everything down and focus on it. Make it start to burn and lift off the launch pad. Go, go, go, go! You have to be intensely focused in order to launch and gain momentum.

Once you reach your destination, you will have a lot more free time to get back into the other things that are important to you. For a while, as Dave Ramsey, the author of *Total Money Makeover*, says, "You will have to live like no one else so later you can live like no one else."

Another trick to keep momentum going is to celebrate small wins with yourself and your team. It is so easy to forget to cheer when we accomplish something. So, at the very beginning of your journey, set small milestones that will help you know when you are approaching and meeting your goal. Then party, praise, and tell everyone involved, including yourself.

I read a book a few years ago called *Whale Done*. The authors discussed the way that killer whales are trained to perform in shows at water parks. The premise is: "How do you get a huge animal like a killer whale to jump 20 feet out of the water when you want it to?" You can't really scold an animal like that; you must praise it and reward it to train it to do what you want. The trainers start by holding a stick between them. They submerge and try to get the whale to go between them and over the stick. If the whale does it correctly, they reward it with fish; if it goes under or around the stick, they ignore it and work to coerce it to go over the stick the way they want it to. Pretty soon, the animal understands the fastest way to the reward is to go over the stick. Once it's an automatic response, the trainers raise the stick up to the water's surface and get the animal to leap out of the water. They continue this process until the whale will leap to incredible heights and put on an amazing show for the crowds.

As I have built my business, I have really benefitted from this type of leadership and motivational thought process: to celebrate the small wins and minimize the faults and failures, not to punish myself when I do something badly. As I have practiced this, I have seen my team reach higher and higher every year to the point where we have become one of the best in the country at what we do. When people come to visit my company they say, "Wow, you have great people. If I could find people like that, then I could build a business like yours, too." But they don't realize that the perfect employees didn't just float down from the sky like Mary Poppins. They are looking at years of training and coaching people in a healthy environment to have them perform like that. To have great performers, you must set the stage for them to perform on.

I have a naturally optimistic outlook on life. I know that not everyone shares that same outlook, but optimism is a core leadership trait that you must project for your company to grow. At one point I told a group that I was in that I see "rainbows and unicorns" as a general theme running in my head. This doesn't mean deluding yourself into thinking that everything is great all the time. You still need to stand up and take charge when a problem occurs or one of your people makes a big mistake. We can acknowledge that these things can and will happen but not be so bothered by them that they run our lives and cause us unnecessary stress.

I believe that I am a realistic person, but I give more weight, in my mind, to the positive and the possibilities than I do to the negative and the doubts. I believe that this optimism also translates into another core leadership value: excitement.

When I am excited about an idea, I can get my team to follow through. The more often that I am correct and follow through on my ideas, the more growth and success we see. Success has great magnetism, so the more successful I am, the more likely people want to be part of something that is winning.

Lastly, when you are winning, remember that opportunities never cease. As you build and create, your confidence will increase and more and more opportunities will come your way. You will be able to see more opportunities, and others will want to have you involved in theirs. As this starts to happen, gravity seems to have a diminished effect on you. It feels totally different than when you first launched the rocket off of the pad, more like you are entering into the upper atmosphere.

As you celebrate all successes, large and small, you will understand that the momentum you are creating has an excitement of its own. Take action now.

Here are a few of my business truths:

1. Every man-made object in the world was once an idea before it became reality. It has to start with you speaking it into existence. If you don't say it, it won't become a reality, guaranteed. You have to see it in your mind's eye and speak about it with everyone you can.

2. If you don't want to have a big business, you won't get one. I have found that this is very common among older business people. Many younger people getting into the service industry are already thinking of .

building larger businesses. It's exciting to work with this mindset instead of trying to teach an old dog new tricks. I hear it all of the time: "I wouldn't want a bigger business like yours." To this I say, "Are you sure about that?" No matter what, if you say that out loud, you have just trained your brain to shut down opportunities.

3. If you don't really care about having a lot of money, you won't get any. In the book *Secrets of the Millionaire Mind*, T. Harv Eker talks about an interesting way that money works. He says that if anyone ever says, "I don't work for money," or "I'm not in this for the money," he's talking to someone who's broke. If you say that out loud, then it's the same as if someone was saying to a friend of theirs, "I don't really like you," or "I'm not concerned about you." Will you be around that person very much? Probably not. Money works the exact same way. Of course, you don't want to make everything about money (greed is a nasty thing), but to be concerned with money and to watch after it is not being greedy; it's being a good steward.

4. If you say employees are a pain in the rear, you won't have many. I have found that it's just like anything else: if you don't like them, they probably don't like you either. I find that it's a lot easier to run my business if I truly care about my employees and they know it. They start to care about me, too, and we move better as a team. It is also easier to make changes with them because we have developed a solid relationship. I won't make a decision without trying to fully understand how the change will affect them. If you generally don't like people, you can still run an effective company as long as you are clear and

balanced. In many cases, you need great employees more than they need you. To build your company, it is a must to cultivate and develop great and loyal employees.

If you can't handle what you have, you won't go to the next level. One of my favorite things to say to myself whenever I'm hitting a wall or when the stress is too much is, "Mark, if you can't handle this business at two million dollars, then you can't handle it at three or four million dollars."

An employee of mine once told me that he wanted to build a real estate business and was going to have about twenty properties in his portfolio. One day he was very distressed and said that he was having a lot of trouble out of his first and only property. The tenants hadn't paid the rent on time, which caused him to have financial problems. Once he moved them out, there was a lot of damage to the home that he had to repair before he could rent it again. I told him that he needed to suck it up and learn from whatever issues occurred and to start working on a way to avoid these issues as he added more properties. Every level that you achieve in business has lessons to learn from before you get to go to the next level. It's almost like a gatekeeper that won't let you pass through until you can manage the problems at your current level.

CHAPTER NINE

Driving While Flying

"Coming together is a beginning; keeping together is progress; working together is success."

—Henry Ford

As I was building my team, I noticed a trend that really disappointed me and made me feel discouraged. The trend was the cars in my parking lot, specifically the number and condition of the vehicles that were amassing outside of my office.

You see, I had about seventeen employees at the time, but only about eight or nine cars in my parking lot. Of those eight or nine cars, six of them were complete junk mobiles. Many of my employees were being brought to work, being picked up by other employees or, even worse, borrowing my vans to get back and forth to work. I remember driving in one day, passing those cars and thinking this was a sign that I was not building a successful company that I could be proud of. I realized that what would make me feel like I was doing the right thing would be to see a parking lot full of nice cars and trucks. I didn't think I could drive up in a nice car or live in a nice home while everyone else was barely scraping by, even though I had already paid my dues and I was the one taking all of the risk. I needed to raise their ability to earn a good living before I could pay myself a high salary. I realized that I wanted them to have an opportunity to make a good living, have homes, take vacations, and save for retirement.

As you build your company and imagine what a successful business looks like, you need to write it down so that you know what it will look and feel like when you get there. It may be a parking lot full of nice cars or a bigger building or better equipment. Visualization can be immensely helpful in targeting what you want out of your business.

Today, my parking lot is full of nice vehicles for the office staff and the technicians, and it feels great to pull into my business. In fact, I have had several job seekers come into my office and ask for an application just because of the nice vehicles parked around the building. It's a sign that I'm running a great and profitable company that can pay its employees what they deserve. Now I can allow myself to have nice things, too, and my employees want me to have them instead of being upset as my lifestyle gets better and theirs doesn't.

As your business becomes more successful, great magnetism can start to build around you and your team. This can be a dangerous thing as your business starts to take flight and soar. You can start to feel almost invincible, thinking all of your decisions are great and that you are a super smart business person. Be very careful as you enter this new world, because neither success nor failure is permanent. Stay grounded in the principles that brought you to this place in life. Stay humble and giving of your time and efforts. Writer Patrick Allen wrote an article on Lifehacker.com about the benefits of being humble in business:

> You've heard it all your life: being humble, kind, and calm is the "right thing to do." But if that isn't enough to convince you, consider this:

humility, kindness, and calmness can actually help you get ahead in life.

Confidence is key to getting ahead in life. It helps you do better at work, in relationships, and in interviews. Overconfidence, however, can make you seem like a genuine jerk. We all know that one person that thinks they are the strongest, smartest, and just all around best at everything. Truthfully, we all dislike that person to some degree.

So while confidence is essential, it's important to stay humble as well (the two aren't as contradictory as you might think). Remember the tale of the Emperor's New Clothes: It's okay to be wrong about something and, more importantly, it's okay to admit that to others. This shows that you not only value your opinion and decisions, but that you also value the opinions and decisions of those around you.

People respond well to humility because it shows that you place yourself at the same level as them, and not above them.

A few years ago I was at a conference. The speaker went through an exercise called "My perfect day," where he described in vivid detail what his perfect day would consist of. Listening to his perfect day was very inspiring to everyone in the crowd, and I have since used it for myself and others to help visualize the future.

One of the best outcomes of this exercise that I have experienced was with an ex-employee of mine we called "Cheeto." He had been an employee with us for many years and was very well liked in the company, but he had a very bad drug problem he couldn't shake. Although he tried year after year to get clean, he never could, and he always fell back into his addiction. It was hard to watch this knowing we couldn't help him. As our strict company drug testing was approaching, he admitted that he had started using again. He went ahead and admitted himself into another drug program, completed it in 90 days, and started to work in a factory when he left.

About six months later a mutual friend of ours was getting married in Ohio, so Cheeto and I decided to ride together to the wedding. Even though it was a five-hour drive, I was looking forward to catching up. He was always a funny guy, and I knew we would laugh the entire trip. As we were driving, he told me how well he was doing, so I asked him what else he wanted in life. He was almost 40 years old and didn't really have anything to show for it at that point: no money, no car, no girlfriend or wife, no home, no kids, no education.

He said, "I don't know. I have never really allowed myself to think about having much. I was always just concerned about surviving." Wow, that hit me like a ton of bricks, and it really helped me to understand his frame of mind.

So I said, "Let's just try it. We have nothing to lose, and it's just a chance to let yourself dream."

He said okay and we started. So here's how the exercise went:

Cheeto: I want a house.

Me: Okay, what kind of house do you want?

Cheeto: Oh, I don't know, a small house I guess.

Me: What kind of small house? A brick house? A log cabin? A ranch style house?

Cheeto: A little brick ranch house.

Me: Good. Where is this house located? Is it in the country or a neighborhood?

Cheeto: The country...with a little pond.

Me: Nice! Okay, is it in Tennessee or somewhere else?

Cheeto: Tennessee for sure.

Me: How much land do you have around the house?

Cheeto: About two acres.

Me: Great, okay. I can see it now. Can you see it, Cheeto?

Cheeto: Yes, I can really see it.

Me: Are you married or have a girlfriend?

Cheeto: Yes, I'm married.

Me: Okay, what does she look like?

Cheeto: Well, she's attractive but not hot, she's a little on the chunky side but overall kind of plain...maybe a six. (We started to laugh out loud.)

Me: Okay, does she work or stay at home?

Cheeto: She works! I can barely afford this dream let alone pay for all of her stuff too! (We were rolling at this point.)

Me: Do you have kids?

Cheeto: Not yet, but we plan to eventually.

Me: What does a perfect day look like?

Cheeto: We get up around 7 a.m. and fix a little breakfast and coffee. We sit out on our porch that overlooks the pond, just relaxing. Then, when we finish breakfast, we go down to the pond with our lawn chairs and start fishing.

Me: Do you catch anything?

Cheeto: We catch some nice small bass, but we throw them all back. Then it would be about time for lunch and she would fix us something.

Me: Okay, what would you do for her?

Cheeto: Just being around me should be enough for her. I mean, come on, look at me! (Again, we were cracking up.)

Me: What kind of vehicle do you drive?.

Cheeto: I drive an older Chevy truck.

Me: What color?

Cheeto: I think dark blue.

I sat there for a minute just thinking.

Me: Wow, I can really see what your life looks like now. Can you?

Cheeto: Definitely! Man, I have never allowed myself to imagine a life like that, but I can see it now and I'm kind of getting excited about it.

We both got a little teared up. He must have said ten times, "Wow, Mark, I can really see it, and I think I can do it!"

I said, "I know you can, for sure."

While you were reading, could you see Cheeto's life with his house and everything? I know you could, and that's what I mean by driving while flying. We were looking at his life from above and zooming in and out of it. It was a lot of fun.

After that, every few months he would reach out to me and say, "Thank you for doing that exercise with me."

About a year later, he called and said, "Guess what? I got a little ranch house!"

I said, "That is so cool."

He then said, "And I have a girlfriend."

I said, "Great job. Is she a six?"

He said, "A five!"

We cracked up, he thanked me again and said that none of it would have happened if I hadn't helped him to see it. That exercise helped him focus while he worked, helped him have a better outlook on life and, I believe, helped him attract a possible life partner because he had a plan, felt confident, and had direction in his life.

Have you ever really looked at what you want in life with that type of vivid detail? Real detail with colors and sounds and smells and location? Can you see how valuable it would be if you took 30 minutes right now and wrote it down as you imagined it? Can you imagine if you really took the time to do it with members of your team?

That's the kind of thing that shows your employees you care about the "why" they are working for you. Many people never let themselves dream too big because it's just too painful if they fail to reach it, or they don't think there is any way they can achieve higher levels of success. This exercise is very simple but can really give them purpose in what they do every day.

1. Do the perfect-day exercise on yourself. Really give it specific details and time frames. The more details, the better.

2. Do the perfect-day exercise for your employees or spouse. Have fun with it.

3. Realize when you are having a perfect or near-perfect day as they happen.

CHAPTER TEN

Exit...Stage Right

"Begin with the end in mind."

—*Peter Drucker*

There are four ways in which people leave their small businesses:

1. Shut the doors and walk away

2. Give it to their kids or employees

3. Sell it to a buyer, employees, or family members

4. Set up a continued payment or salary plan. They continue to draw money as an owner's share after they leave the business.

I'm sure there are others, but I haven't seen them happen. People often forget about their exit strategy when they are starting out as it seems too far away and irrelevant or isn't nice to think about. But how are you going to get there if you don't know where "there" is? A simple exit strategy will give you direction. Remember the earlier story about how I couldn't sell my business when I wanted to get out of it? I might have been able to avoid that scenario if I had planned my exit a little better. It worked out well in the end, but it caused me a lot of struggle and headaches.

The smaller things tend to fall into place much more easily when the bigger things have already been decided.

Your exit strategy can be a very powerful motivator because you know that you are working with a plan and specific goal in mind. When you set the exit strategy in place, it will help you get through the rough times. Rather than wrecking your business, those rough times become more like bumps in the road while you are headed toward the big pay day at the end. The exit strategy will help put your issues into perspective. As I grew my business, what were big issues when I was running a smaller company weren't such a big deal as I saw how they really played out.

Knowing when and how you will sell your business can help you think about what you need to do (and by when) to maximize your business's value for your planned exit point.

Being aware of the prospect of selling your business allows you to think about and focus on the activity that will achieve the greatest value at the point you intend to sell. You can understand how to value your small business and take the steps that will make it worth more to potential buyers.

It's always better to have the luxury of time when going through the business sale process as you can wait out for the best offer. If you want to sell and get out quickly, then you'll be inclined to accept the first offer that comes along, which may not always be the most profitable one or may force you to make a bad decision out of desperation.

When I was laid up with damaged legs and tried and failed to sell my business, I learned a very hard lesson. I didn't really have a business to sell; I was really trying to sell a "job." There is a big difference between the two, and I was about to learn it. Nobody wants to buy a job. They want to buy a business.

The difference was easy to see, but hard to change. A job-type business is one that can't function without the owner or one key person. This person is mission critical, and most decisions and work are done by them. So, if they were gone, the business would fall into chaos or stop functioning. The second type of company is more along the lines of what most people would think of as a business. It can run mostly without the owner being present. These definitions make a huge difference in the value of a business to potential buyers, because most of them are not looking to actually do the work itself; they want a business they can manage that flings off cash.

A book that everyone in a service business needs to read is *The E-Myth Revisited* by Michael Gerber. This book changed my direction and business life.

When I discovered this, I began to change the type of business I was creating—I set up a company that I could eventually sell for more money. At one point, a mentor of mine said, "Mark, the business that you really want to own is one that you can get away from and doesn't need you to run." That was some of the best business advice that I have ever heard. If you start making your business decisions to build this type of company, it will change your trajectory and how you think of getting out of your business from that day forward.

I will list the steps that I took to make this fundamental change:

1. You must read and study as much as you can about leadership. This has been the best thing that I have

ever done for myself and all of those who have come to work for me.

2. Determine what you do on a daily basis and begin to turn these daily tasks into a job that someone else can do. Hire someone to do this job or give it to someone in your company.

3. Repeat steps one and two over and over until you are a great leader. You don't want to have any daily tasks that must be completed by you and no one else.

As you do this, you can test your systems and people by leaving on vacations for weeks and even months at a time. When you return from each of these absences, take note as to the breakdowns that occurred and work to fix them. For me, it was usually a break down in leadership because while I had been working to make myself a great leader I wasn't transferring that knowledge to my team. Once you recognize and fix these mistakes, you'll find that the business will run automatically even while you're not there.

It took me about two years to really turn my company into a business that could work without me on a daily basis. After that, it took another two to three years to make it so that I could be gone for an extended period of time. This change in how my company runs has been life changing for me in many ways, and my business no longer feels like a chain around my neck. Plus, my business continues to make money whether I am there or not.

The main component of my exit strategy is to make my business run completely autonomously, and I will continue to take a weekly or monthly owner's draw from the profits. I work every day with that exit strategy in mind but, as we all know, plans change. I'm making my business as strong as possible so that I have other good exit options should I need them.

You also need to plan how the business will be taken care of if something were to happen to you, the owner. A multitude of misfortunes can befall you, including prolonged illness or injury that leaves you physically or mentally unable to run the company, or even death. Nobody likes to consider these things happening but, unfortunately, they do happen and there is no avoiding them. You need a contingency plan.

Many of the exercises that were discussed earlier will apply if you are sick or injured, but your salary and your plan must be made in writing. As you start to develop these ideas, you should enlist an attorney to help you with all of these contingency plans. You must also let your spouse and anyone related to the management of your company know of your plans.

I have found that the "death scenario" has a few more pieces to it. First, your will needs to be in order and updated annually. Second, purchase a key-man policy. This was one of my first purchases from my insurance agent. If you don't know what these are, please consult your insurance agent about them. Basically, they are a life insurance policy that you take out on any key person in your business, including yourself. These pay back to a beneficiary to be used for continuation of your business in case something bad happens. This policy will provide money to hire a person or people to help in the interim until the business can recover from the loss.

I have also taken the step to appoint a board of people to find a replacement for me if I should become incapacitated or die. I asked two of my mentors, one close business advisor and my general manager to interview and find an acceptable replacement for me.

These people know me very well, and they know the kind of culture and core values we have at my company. I have full faith that they will do an outstanding job of taking care of my company if I can't. We have all heard of the complete disasters businesses experience when the owner passes on or is no longer in charge. Many times this results from a failure in leadership from the owner. They didn't set up a structure that the company would thrive under. The best leaders hand off the business to someone who can take it to new heights. I have personally witnessed a close friend's business implode when he tried to hand off the business to his employees.

My friend was diagnosed with terminal cancer, and the doctors told him he only had months to live. He actually beat the expectations and lived for another two years. He ended up having plenty of time to make the transition as smooth as possible. He handled much of it correctly, but he didn't listen to his counsel about how to transition the business to four key employees. We advised that four was too many and that it would be better to sell the business to only one of them or to an outside buyer.

My friend was adamant about handing it off to his employees, however, so we went ahead and worked with that scenario. The biggest problem was that he picked a supreme A-hole of a guy to be the president in charge of the other owners. I couldn't stand this guy from the moment I met him. None of his advisors liked him. Unfortunately, he was showing my friend his best face and he couldn't see what we were seeing, so he made his decision final.

The new owners took over while he was still alive, though he still had a guiding hand as they did. When he died, the new team started to show its true colors, and we saw bad signs right off the bat. Within two years, the company was broke and they had major internal turmoil. In year three the partners voted to remove the president and elect a new one. Since then they have started to reestablish their company. I believe that they will be fine now, but they came far too close to shutting down completely. As you plan for your exit, make sure you stage it right.

To recap your exit plan:

1. Write down your plan A and plan B.

2. Let your key people know what the plan is.

3. Consult with an attorney.

4. Consult with an insurance agent about a key-man policy.

CHAPTER ELEVEN

Why You Won't Change Anything

"I've learned that people will forget what you said,
people will forget what you did,
but people will never forget how you made them feel."

—*Maya Angelou*

There is a great lesson about success and leadership to be learned from studying the way that buffalo and cows respond to storms. Rory Vaden's book, *Take the Stairs*, tells about the instinctual reactions of both cows and buffalo on the plains of Colorado when a storm is seen coming over the mountains.

Colorado, where he grew up, is famous for the Rocky Mountains. What a lot of people don't realize, however, is that the state is divided almost exactly in half. In the eastern half of the state are the plains of Kansas. Because of this unique landscape, it is one of the few places in the world where both buffalo and cows live in close proximity.

When storms come to Colorado, they almost always brew from the west and move toward the east.

When cows sense the storm coming from the west, their natural reaction is to run toward the east. The only problem with this is that cows aren't very fast, so the storm catches up with them rather quickly. Without knowing any better, the cows continue trying to outrun the storm. But instead of outrunning the storm, they actually run right along with it, maximizing the amount of pain, time, and frustration they experience from the storm.

What buffalo do, on the other hand, is unique in the animal kingdom. Buffalo wait for the storm to crest over the peak of the mountaintop, and as the storm rolls over the ridge, the buffalo turn and charge directly into it. Instead of running east, away from the storm, they run west, directly at it. By doing so, they minimize the amount of pain, time, and frustration they experience from that storm.

This is a great metaphor for many business and life challenges. Humans act like the cows all of the time. They spend so much of their lives trying to avoid the inevitable challenges of the difficult circumstances created by their own choices. So "buffalo up" when you are faced with challenges. Identify them and go right through them as quickly as possible. Many times they aren't nearly as bad as you had imagined. One of my biggest "cow" situations is when I need to fire someone. I always want to figure out a way to keep them on, and any excuse they have will do for me. This has infuriated many great people on my team when they are doing a great job but I'm keeping someone that makes their job and life much more difficult. I have learned to be the buffalo and to take action much more quickly to preserve our culture and to not burn out my good people.

I have personally consulted with nearly 500 small business owners and spoken to many thousands of people in seminars throughout the years. It is frustrating that the most common reaction to my advice and teachings is to do absolutely nothing. What makes my heart sing is when people are fired up to practice my advice and actually start to move and gain momentum.

In order to grow my business faster, I have surrounded myself with mentors and coaches. I believe that this is one of the best practices to leapfrog your way through the problems you will encounter.

One of my first mentors was an icon in the chimney service area named John Meredith. He was already a thriving business owner when I met him in 2006; we seemed to have an instant connection. I felt like this guy really cared about me. I later realized that he just has that amazing character trait to instantly connect with people and to truly care about them. I immediately started seeing how he spread this to anyone who knew him.

I can clearly recall the first time I met John. It was during a conference we were both attending and we were playing blackjack in the hotel casino between scheduled events. Eventually, we left the table and as we walked and talked I witnessed him slipping $25 chips into the shirt pockets and palms of people that he knew. He had won about $250 and proceeded to give it all away.

I thought, *Wow, how cool is that!*

Later that night he invited me to dinner with a large group to an excellent restaurant. As the dinner progressed, he stood and walked all around the table and spoke with everyone. When the dinner was finished, he picked up the bill for everyone, including me, whom he had just met. I was blown away by his generosity, and it taught me a great lesson about the principle of Givers Gain.

John and I stayed in touch, and about a year later he called me to join a test group working on a new project that he was developing for repairing chimneys. At this time my business was crumbling, and I was almost broke. When he asked me to look into purchasing the equipment to start using this new repair method, I told him the truth about my financial situation. Being the type of guy he is, he told me not to worry, that he would provide everything I needed to start this new method. He was showing me the way as a mentor, and I wasn't going to let him down. Over the next couple of years, as I dug myself out of my financial pit, I became the largest dealer of his new product in the U.S. He later recommended me for a director position for the Chimney Safety Institute of America, for which I later became president. John has also helped me with numerous other ideas and lessons with my business, and I can say without a doubt that I would not be in the position that I am in now without his influence and mentorship.

I believe that you too need to find a mentor for your journey. A mentor needs to be a successful business person who has your best interest in mind. This is not someone whom you are paying for advice; that would be a coach. While coaches are effective, they aren't the same as mentors. A mentor will tell you how it is and not sugarcoat it; they will cheer for you when you win and give you sound advice whenever you are approaching danger or have crashed and need help. They can be a family member, but I feel that a successful business person with a helpful and supportive attitude will prove more effective.

When you begin to work with mentors and coaches, you need to remember one incredibly important thing: DO WHAT THEY SAY! I see it all of the time when people visit me. From the questions they ask and the notes they take, I can almost immediately tell if they're going to take my advice or not.

Sometimes you may not feel brave enough to change your life. Change can be scary. Doing things for the first time or stepping into the unknown can be pretty frightening. You may feel like you need some courage to make those changes you want, to take those first steps.

As Eleanor Roosevelt once said, "You gain strength, courage and confidence by every experience in which you really stop to look fear in the face. You are able to say to yourself, 'I have lived through this horror. I can take the next thing that comes along.' You must do the thing you think you cannot do."

You have to be willing to take action, to move out of your comfort zone, and to face fear to increase your courage and self-confidence in a way that stays with you.

You have to be willing to take the punch and risk some emotional pain for a while. There is no way of getting around that.

I won't lie to you. Sometimes it will suck. You will go to bed feeling sick to your stomach and just pray for the day to end.

Well, the next day you will wake up. You will realize that you are still here. You are intact and the earth keeps spinning, and you will get up for a new day. Life continues. But now you know deep down that you can handle problems at least a little bit better because you could handle what happened yesterday. You have raised your confidence in yourself and become stronger.

Many nights you will go to bed feeling great for passing that invisible barrier and facing your fear. You may not always get the desired result, but you can still feel great about yourself because you still dared to face that fear or take some action.

When you work through problems, you don't only build confidence in your ability, you also experience progressive desensitization. For example, if public speaking terrifies you, continue to give speeches to make it increasingly easier. This is what I meant earlier by getting on stage and keep getting on stage. You'll never learn how to perform if you never step onto the stage, and performing on the stage is the only way that you will get better at it. Over time it will become as natural as tying your shoes, hanging out with your friends, or taking a shower. You'll find that you don't need much courage to do it after a while.

The other way of getting help is to look into a franchise to speed up your process. As I mentioned earlier in the book, I recently started a chimney business franchise called SirVent Chimney and Venting (sirventfranchising.com). We worked for about two years creating what we needed for our operations manual, our franchise disclosure documents, a full marketing plan, website, legal documents, and training program with videos. We recently sold our first franchise in Charlotte, North Carolina.

Another possibility we found for us to expand is to convert existing businesses to our model and to help them get to the next level. Business owners often can't seem to move their business forward, but we believe that they will like our system and that our knowledge of building businesses will help them if they join our team. If you are looking to start a new business and want to speed up your results and increase your chances for success, you may want to consider a pre-existing franchise in your area of interest.

If you are serious about starting a business, you would be taking notes, highlighting, or at least dog earring pages while reading this book, right? Be honest; what did you do? If you want to start a business or are trying to take yours to the next level, why haven't you done it yet?

I hope my experiences are something you can learn from; if not, I hope you found some useful nugget of information in this book regardless. If you are serious about your business and believe that this book helped you, go back and highlight the good stuff (unless you borrowed the book or got it from a library, of course), and even re-read the book a few times over the next few months, as you won't be able to remember everything by heart.

You will be surprised how much you missed the first time that you can use later.

One of the neatest things for me to see in business is a person on fire in their thoughts and actions who executes their ideas and goals. I can always hear it in their voices and see it in their eyes when they are speaking to me. Just today, as I am writing this book, my friend Kevin contacted me about a dilemma that he is having. See, Kevin is absolutely on fire for his new business and has been this way for about two years. His business is really starting to gain momentum and make great strides. He is also building his business in a way which allows him to do what he is truly passionate about—using his horse farm as a healing facility for veterans with PTSD. I love his mission, so anything that I can do to help him, I will.

He emailed me and asked about a work/life balance issue he is having. As I stated earlier, your life will be put on a back burner while you are initially building your business. He said, "Mark, I'm getting ready to go on an anniversary cruise with my wife, but I still have a lot of work to do right now and it will be hard to set it down for ten days while I'm gone. What should I do? Work or relax?"

You may totally disagree with my advice, but here's what I said: "Kevin, when you are launching a rocket, you must focus on that launch. Once you get your ship into orbit, you can work on getting in balance with everything else. Go on the cruise and spend time with your wife, but I would still be working instead of doing nothing. Keep the momentum up unless you are getting burned out."

In my experience, staying focused on a project I'm excited about is far better for my mind than trying to turn it off. I actually feel more stressed when I can't or don't do the work I know I should be doing.

CHAPTER TWELVE

Solutions

*"Twenty years from now you will be more
disappointed by the things that you didn't do than by
the ones you did so throw off the bowlines. Sail away
from the safe harbor. Catch the trade winds in your
sails. Explore. Dream. Discover."*

—*Mark Twain*

One of my favorite stories is about how gutsy Sir Richard Branson was when he started Virgin Airlines:

> I was in my late twenties, so I had a business, but nobody knew who I was at the time. I was headed to the Virgin Islands and I had a very pretty girl waiting for me, so I was, umm, determined to get there on time.

> At the airport, my final flight to the Virgin Islands was cancelled because of maintenance or something. It was the last flight out that night. I thought this was ridiculous, so I went and chartered a private airplane to take me to the Virgin Islands, which I did not have the money to do.

Then, I picked up a small blackboard, wrote "Virgin Airlines. $29." on it, and went over to the group of people who had been on the flight that was cancelled. I sold tickets for the rest of the seats on the plane, used their money to pay for the chartered plane, and we all went to the Virgin Islands that night.

Richard Branson also has one of my favorite business mottos as well. It's "Screw it, let's do it!"

This final chapter covers what to do when starting over in business or starting a business for the first time. I have started many businesses and learned a lot from every single one, so I will do my best to help you get started or get moving. If you have ever wanted to start a business, you couldn't be in a better place or a better time in history. If you have already started a business but it isn't growing as much or as quickly as you would like, these should hopefully get you on the right path.

1. Implement now, perfect later

This is the best concept in business that I can encourage you to do. There is a story about a college art class that had an assignment to make pottery for their final grade for the semester. The professor split the class in half and gave each half slightly different assignments. He told one half of the class that their grade was dependent on turning in just one piece of pottery at the end of the semester. It needed to be as perfect as it could be. They could spend the entire semester on only one fantastic pot. The other half of the class was told to turn in as many pots as they could make and they would be graded on the weight of the pots turned in. It didn't matter what they looked like, the more pots the students turned in, the better their grades would be.

A funny thing happened by the end of the semester. The half of the class that had to turn in quantity turned in higher quality pots than the other half. The mere act of going through the motions over and over made them better at it than the other half, which was only trying to make one.

2. Read books, or at least listen to books. (I know I have said it a lot in this book!)

Not just leadership, self-help or motivational books, but any book that has new ideas will do. Learning new ideas puts your brain in motion, so you will require less time to speed up to your tasks. It must become a daily activity for you. Imagine if you read one leadership or business book a month—that's 12 books a year. What a different business person you would become in just one year. What if you keep it up over five years and put 72 books into your brain? Books are so easily accessible today; we have iBooks, Kindle, and Nook apps, and even Audible for times when we can't read but can listen. If you don't read very often and find it difficult to start, then don't worry. Start off slowly, perhaps with just a chapter or a few pages every night. The evening is usually the best time to read. Even just a few pages every day all add up over time. You don't even have to try everything you read all at once. Take each exercise or tip one at a time and see which ones work for you.

I started reading on a continuous basis when I was 34, and what I learned about leadership was priceless for my business. I'm very glad that I learned so many key principles and developed the habit of reading. It became one of the biggest keys to my growth.

3. Don't be afraid to make mistakes, just make new ones

Doing something the wrong way is at least ten times more productive than doing nothing at all. Every success has a trail of failures behind it, and every failure can be leading towards success. You will end up regretting the things you did NOT do far more than the things you did.

My friend and business coach, Jerry Isenhour of CVC Coaching, has a groundhog as the mascot for his business. The groundhog represents the trap that many business owners fall into—repeating the same mistakes again and again, just like in the movie *Groundhog Day*. In that movie, Bill Murray's character wakes up every day and re-lives the exact same day, making the same mistakes over and over until he gets it right. Many business owners sometimes fall into a funk and let the same issues happen over and over again. This kind of Groundhog Day loop in your business will absolutely burn you out and waste an unbelievable amount of time and money. Always look at your problems and develop a culture of not accepting such a waste in your business.

There are many inspiring stories of growth to inspire you. Colonel Sanders didn't found KFC until he was 65. Coca-Cola sold 25 bottles in their first year and now sell 1.9 billion servings a day around the world. Successful companies aren't those that did everything perfectly the first time around; they are the ones that remained persistent and stuck with it. The most important thing is to learn from your failure rather than repeat it.

4. Stop thinking you're not ready

The biggest reason why "now" is the right time is because "later" almost never is. You can wait yourself into old age and regret, but you don't need to. Even if your business doesn't work, it won't be the end of your life.

When you launch your business, it's best to have an emergency backup plan for how you will support yourself if your business fails, whether it be your savings, your partner's income, or returning to full-time employment. If this does happen, it is discouraging, but you don't need to see it as the end of everything. It's just a temporary ditch that you will climb out of.

Nobody ever feels 100 percent ready when an opportunity arises. Most great opportunities in life force us to grow beyond our comfort zones, which means we won't feel totally comfortable at first. It's essential to understand that there is no "right time" to launch a new business. There is no ideal economic environment, no perfect market window, no flawless product idea that will guarantee your new business will be a success. But America is primed and in need of more blue-collar service businesses. In my opinion, the American economy couldn't be in a better place for you to move forward with your plans. The right time is when you're ready. Don't look for outside indications to tell you when to launch your own business. Look inside to your own desires and commitment. Launch when you cannot not launch, and don't get hung up on the externals.

I'm not saying you should immediately quit your job, re-mortgage your house, and buy a factory to launch your dream. I am saying you shouldn't use your existing commitments as excuses not to start. As I've said throughout this book, planning is important. If you plan correctly, then you won't have to sit around and wait for the perfect time. You'll be putting your resignation notice onto your boss's desk, going to your own desk and becoming you own boss!

5. Stop following the path of least resistance

Life is not easy, especially when you plan on achieving something worthwhile. Don't take the easy way out. Do something extraordinary. Voltaire once said, "The enemy of the great is the good." What's great about this quote is that it doesn't end the way you think it would. You would think it would say that the enemy of the great is the bad or the evil, but he says it's the good. When you really think about it, you won't go for the great if you already have it good. If you are comfortable, you probably won't stretch to go for something greater. But is that what you want for your life? Comfortable? A comfortable life and financial stability are great, but it is far too easy to settle into a life that is comfortable but nothing else. It is another thing that can be used as an excuse to never try for more. I always feel a little uncomfortable, and I want to see if I can push through to the next level.

6. Use technology—it has become cheaper and easier
    to obtain

Any modern business needs technology. Relying on outdated tools or marketing methods will cause your business to slow down and eventually stop altogether. You'll need customer relationship management, accounting, a website and email hosting, and possibly design software or other tools. Cloud computing provides needed services on a monthly basis without laying out too much cash at the start. Also, hardware is relatively cheap, so getting an upgraded PC or tablet won't cost a body part or two.

I discussed websites, social media, and other computer technology earlier in this book because they are important. Technology is always changing and developing, which is great, but it can be hard to keep up and sometimes overwhelming to constantly familiarize yourself with something new. But you will have to buck up and do it because it could make the difference between success and failure for your business. It doesn't really need to be that difficult. Just read a few technology blogs, keep your website updated, and watch out for new social media trends. (Your younger friends or relatives will be a great help with this!)

Don't become fixated on one piece of technology just because you have grown used to it. It can be frustrating to constantly learn about new technology, but it is just another one of those things you have to do. Eventually you'll realize that is the best thing for your business too.

7. Support on the home front

I have been married twice, and I have had two completely different experiences when it comes to spousal support. In the beginning, my first wife was very supportive of my business and my music. We had only been married for about three years when the stress of a new business and two little children led to an unsupportive atmosphere. I remember that my wife at the time couldn't handle the ebbs and flows of a new business and my income being so unstable. She wanted me to get a "real job" to support us, but I knew that that wasn't going to happen unless all else failed. That level of stress in the home made building a business very difficult.

Unfortunately, my first marriage ended in divorce and was financially devastating for me. I lost half of my business, my home, and my family in one bad situation. It took me several years to dig out of the mess, but I finally began to pull out of it when I married Terry. As of the writing of this book, we have been married for eleven years, and she has remained incredibly supportive of all my endeavors. This has allowed me to walk the tightrope and push the envelope of my business because she always has my back. I have seen many couples work together as a great team for years, but I have also seen many couples run into trouble.

I know that many entrepreneurs are in an unsupportive atmosphere, so I have included some tips from business blogger Sophie Gold, posted on Huffingtonpost.com:

1. **Less talking, more action:** Words mean nothing; it's all about the bottom line. Every month share your profit and forecast for the next month.

2. **Everyone wants to feel included**: Don't hide what you are doing, once a week why not tell your loved one what's new in your business.

3. **Let your loved one help:** What skill does your loved one have that could add to the business, sometimes they just want to help, and it goes back to point 2 about being included. If your loved one is an accountant let him do your accounts.

4. **Don't be a seminar junkie:** If there is something that turns off a loved one more than anything it is about hearing the latest quick fix course that is going to solve your problems. There is nothing wrong with working with coaches- I am a coach myself- but if every day you are talking about working with someone else then that is a major turn off. Why not instead do some research, write a list of all your weak points and find a coach or seminar that can help you in your weak areas. Then once your research is complete present your findings to your loved one.

5. **Share the vision:** Paint the picture, talk to your loved one about how happy running your business makes you feel, tell your loved one what your 12 month, 3-year and 5-year vision is.

6. **Don't put down your loved one:** Don't be negative. You have to understand they love you and also they have insecurities. When they say something you don't like listen and then say what you want to say.

7. **Focus on how good it will feel when your loved one is supporting you:** It's easy to call your loved one names, why not instead focus on how great it will feel when your spouse is supporting you. Remember that what you focus on you get. The more you focus on the arguments you have, the more arguments you will have.

   Being an entrepreneur is not a *dirty secret*, and should not be treated as one.

   Based on my own personal experience my spouse was only unsupportive when I didn't communicate effectively with him, but once I did he changed and now he is so supportive and helps me in any way that he can.

   Speak up, share, include and watch the transformation- not just your business but in your relationship.

When I read these words on her blog I felt that her information was spot on and could possibly help any entrepreneurs who have a spouse who throws a wet blanket on their business-building fire.

On one level, it is understandable why a partner would pressure you into getting a "proper" job, especially if you also have children to support. Use good communication like you would with your employees, let your spouse know that you are not running a business for fun or for a hobby—that it *is* your "real job"—and that you are doing it to support your family and provide better for them. Let them know about your plans, including your back-up plan should you fail, and they will know you are taking your business seriously.

So, what's next?

If you are in the blue-collar field or considering it, I want to congratulate you and I hope you found this book helpful. There really is a blue-collar gold out there for you and I want you to find it for yourself. America is going to go through a resurgence of the need for people and companies to take care of their businesses, homes and even themselves, and you can benefit from it.

If there is anyway I can help please reach out to me.

There are a few ways to move forward if you want to join the Blue-Collar-Gold Movement:

If you would like more information about our chimney business franchise opportunity, you can visit www.sir-vent.com. All of the principles in this book are already in action, and I will be one of your coaches to build the service business of your dreams.

Go to www.bluecollargold.com for valuable and trusted resources to help you expand your business.

If you are in a current association that needs a keynote or breakout session speaker, please email me at mark@markstoner. com.

Thank you!

ABOUT THE AUTHOR

Mark Stoner has been in the chimney industry for thirty years. He ran a one-truck company for eighteen years until 2003 when he changed his path and built a multimillion-dollar chimney company only a few years later. Ashbusters Chimney Service currently employs thirty-five people operating sixteen trucks and is currently servicing Middle Tennessee, Southern Kentucky, and Charleston, South Carolina. Mark is the current president of the Chimney Safety Institute of America (CSIA), is the past CSIA vice president and treasurer, and has also served as the National Chimney Sweep Guild Ethics Committee Chairman. Mark was a finalist in the 2012 Nashville NEXT Entrepreneur of the Year award. In 2014, he and three close business partners launched SirVent Chimney and Venting Franchise (www.sir-vent.com). Franchises are available throughout the U.S.